HILDA MARIE BARTON

There's

No

Room

for

Doubt

The just shall live by faith

Order this book online at www.trafford.com
or email orders@trafford.com

Most Trafford titles are also available at major online book retailers.

Printed in the United States of America.

ISBN: 978-1-4269-6401-5 (sc)
ISBN: 978-1-4269-6402-2 (e)

Trafford rev. 04/26/2011

 www.trafford.com

North America & international
toll-free: 1 888 232 4444 (USA & Canada)
phone: 250 383 6864 ♦ fax: 812 355 4082

Acknowledgment

I'd like to dedicate this book to my loving husband,
Leon.
He has been so faithful and helpful to me as I have
spent
many hours and days writing this book and
getting it ready.

He is such a man of faith and love and has inspired
me over
the years. He has such love for Jesus Christ, for me and
our children. He loves the work of the Lord and is
faithful to it.

Together we make such a good team and I thank God
for him. Thank you honey for standing by me and
being so patient with me.

HILDA MARIE BARTON

There's

No

Room

for

Doubt

The just shall live by faith

Table of Contents

Acknowledgment v

Chapter 1 : There is No Room for Doubt................................... 1

Chapter 2 : You Cannot Serve Two Masters................................ 9

Chapter 3 : Keep Yourselves from This Evil Generation 19

Chapter 4 : Truth Causes Division 27

Chapter 5 : Good Can Come Out of Affliction 45

Chapter 6 : Do You need To Change Your Oil? 55

Chapter 7 : From The Beginning it Was Not So....................... 65

Chapter 8 : Preparations For Blessings 73

Chapter 9 : Perennial Or Annual Christian 83

Chapter 10 : We Can Do All Things Through Christ Jesus 97

Chapter 11 : God Takes care of His Children Forever..................... 107

Chapter 12 : Your House Can And Will Stand Strong in Battles....... 115

Chapter 13 : Life Is Tough But God Is Faithful............................. 123

Chapter 14 : The Cure is Jesus Christ 135

Chapter 15 : The River of Life, the Living Water 143

Chapter 16 : We are in a fight.. 151

Chapter 17 : You Are A Slave To Whom You Serve.......................... 165

Chapter 18 : Sin Begins In The Thoughts Of Your Mind................. 171

Chapter 19 : Replace Doubt for Faith... 177

Conclusion..181

About the Author 183

Chapter 1

There is No Room for Doubt

*A*ll prophesies God proclaimed have been proven to be right, so why do you doubt? If God said it, it will come to pass. There is no room for doubt.

Isa.7:14, Therefore the Lord Himself will give you a sign. Behold a virgin shall conceive and bear a Son and shall call His name Emmanuel. 9:6-7, For unto us a child is born, unto us a Son is given and the government shall be upon His shoulders and His name shall be called Wonderful, Counselor, the Mighty God, the everlasting Father and the Prince of Peace. Of the increase of His government and peace shall be no end. The Lord of host shall perform it.

Isa.28:16, The Lord God said, Behold I lay in Zion for a foundation a stone, a tried stone, a precious stone, a sure foundation and he that believes shall never be dissatisfied or dismayed. This is Jesus Christ that he is talking about. Jer.25:5 Behold the days come says the Lord that I will raise into David a righteous Branch and a King shall reign and prosper and execute judgment and justice on earth. This is Jesus that the prophet Jeremiah is prophesying about.

Micah 5:2, Out of Bethlehem shall come forth One who is to be Ruler of Israel whose going forth has been from old to everlasting. This is Jesus Christ our Savior. Zech. 3:8, I will bring forth my servant, the Branch Jesus Christ. 6: 12-13, The One called Branch, Jesus Christ shall build the Lord's temple and shall rule and reign upon God's throne. He shall be a Priest forever. 9:9, Rejoice in Zion, the King comes. He is just and having salvation, lowly and riding on an ass and upon a colt. Just as the prophet Zechariah prophesied it all happened. All of this came to pass in the New Testament. You can read about the birth of Jesus in Luke chapter 2. What was prophesied many years ago happened just as it was prophesied by God through the prophets. Nothing changed from how it was told to the prophets from God. Even in Matt. 21:3, you can read about the prophesy that came to pass when Jesus told His disciples to go into the village and get an ass tied with a colt and bring it to Him. This was done so that it might be fulfilled which was spoken by the prophet saying, behold the King comes to you meek and sitting on as ass and a colt the foul of the ass. This all happened before the crucifixion of Jesus. Zech.12:10, I will pour the house of David and upon the inhabitants of Jerusalem the Spirit of grace and of supplications and they shall look upon Me whom they have pierced and they shall mourn for Him as mourns for his only son and shall be in bitterness for Him as one in bitterness for his first born.

Jesus predicts His own suffering

Mark 8:31, Jesus began to teach them how the Son of man must suffer and die and after three days rise again. This was the resurrection and we know it came to pass. Rom.14:9, Christ died and rose again on the third day. John 2; 19, Jesus said, destroy this temple in three days and I will raise it up. His body was destroyed but not His Spirit. He rose up like He said He would in three days. He was flesh and blood just like you and I but He was also God in the flesh. He died to take the keys to death and hell from the devil to free us from the fear of death. He made an atonement for all of our sins. Those who accept Him and are born again and follow Him will be forgiven and live forever with Him. Through His death and resurrection we have life more abundantly here and life forever in the Kingdom of God. Just as Jesus knew of His death and sufferings He knows what each and everyone will be going through here. If we follow Him we will also suffer with Him. If we deny Him then He will deny us before the Father in Heaven. He knows when we will die just as He knew how and when He was going to die. Our very hairs on our head are numbered. He knew us before we were born and still in our mother's womb. He is Alpha and Omega, the beginning and the end. He is the all knowing God and He's everywhere at the same time. He is Omnipresent and Omnipotent, meaning that He is everywhere, and all powerful and has unlimited power and has all authority over everything everyone.

Our future has been prophesied

It has been proven in God's Word the prophesies of God has come to pass so why or how can you doubt the future prophesies? It's been enough to have already come to pass for us to never doubt the prophesies for the future to come to pass and believe God's Word. It's been appointed for man to die once and then the judgment. We will see that there will be some that will never die for they will be taken up in the rapture of the church. Matt.8:31, Verily, Verily, I say unto you. There will some be standing here that shall never taste of death until they see the Son of man coming in His Kingdom. Now this is the rapture of the church. The church will be caught away to meet Him in the clouds to meet Him in the air. The dead in Christ will rise first and they will be caught away to meet Him in the air all together. Those who have died in faith believing in the Lord Jesus Christ and that they would rise again to be with him are the dead in Christ. You can read all about this in I Thessalonians 4:16-17. He said to comfort each other with these Words in verse 18. You have to ready at all times because no one knows the day or the hour when He is coming back or the day or hour one will leave this world through death. We believe that it will happen in the near future because all of the prophesies have been fulfilled. We can see by the signs of the time that it is near the door. If you're not ready and have your life in order according to His will then you will miss the rapture. If you miss the rapture then you will have to go through the great tribulation that's taught in the Word of God. You do not want to be left here after the church has been taken out. You think you are having or seeing bad time now, you've seen nothing that's going to compare with the time then. It's going to be a time like never before or will ever happen again. Read and study the Bible and you will learn all about these things that's coming to pass. You don't want to miss the great event of the rapture of the church that's coming soon. Be ready and don't miss out on all of the wonderful blessings that God has for His children.

Luke 22; 30, You will eat and drink at my table in My Kingdom. Jesus has been through and done everything that has been prophesied of Him, so why doubt what He says will happen in the future. John 14:2-4, Jesus said, I go to prepare a place for you and I will come again to receive you unto Myself that where I am you will be also. There are many mansions in My Father's Kingdom. And when I go you know and the way you know. There is no reason not to know because He has shown us the way. All you have to do is believe and not doubt and follow Him. Jesus said, I will come again in verse 3. He's coming after a people that are watching and waiting for Him and who are ready to go with Him. Verse 6, Jesus said, I am the way the truth and the life and no one comes to the Father except by Me. He has told the world who He is in His Word, the Bible. From the beginning of the world He has been teaching the same message. He never changes and His prophesies never change. What He has predicted will come to pass. The Bible is the true Word of God, it's not just a fable as some believe. It's not just another book, it's the Word of God. **It is the Book**

Prophecy of the Jews and the fulfillment of this prophecy

Luke 21:24, And they shall fall by the edge of the sword and shall be led into captivity into all nations. Some have seen this happen. They are scattered all over the world. The tribes are scattered everywhere. God told them they would become a byword among all nations. He told Israel that she would be led away captive out of their own land. God told them that He would smite them and root them up out of their land and would scatter them because of their sins and unbelief. We know this all happened because it is written in the Word in the Old Testament. We also, can see the Jews all over the world and how most of the world hates them. God told them they would become a byword. They're still God's chosen people but they have to pay for their sins just as we have to pay for our sins. Deut. 30:3, Then the Lord your God will return captivity and have compassion on you and will return and gather you from all nations where God has scattered you. Jer.16:15, I will bring them again into the land where I gave unto their fathers. The Jews will return again to Israel. Jer.23:3, I will gather the remnant of the flock out of all the nations again. Lots of the Jews have already returned since then and became a nation again. Many of us did not see this but we have read about it so we know it's true because it was prophesied many long years before and now we have seen the second part of the prophesy where they have become a nation again. It's all in the Word of God and no one should ever doubt it. If you will read and study then you will see it too.

There are many other prophesies in the Bible but these are just a few, but enough for you to know and believe they're true and have come and you need to be ready. Are you ready? This is the most important question you can ask yourself. Matt. 24:44, He said He was coming back at a time you're not looking for Him, at the hour you'd least expect Him. I Cor.15:52, He will come in the twinkling of an eye. We're to live holy, clean, sanctified, and keep our heart and life in order at all times. Believe on the Lord Jesus Christ and you shall be saved. Don't doubt!

Who Do You Trust?

When you're depressed, when you're busy beyond belief, when life dishes out its challenges, where do you turn to, and to whom? Where do you put your trust? Often a friend, a parent, a spouse, a colleague, a pastor or a counselor maybe? Sometimes people turn to food, alcohol, drugs, cigarettes, sex or other things that are a quick fix that will dull their senses for just a little while. Unfortunately, these pain killers whether they are labeled good or bad for us don't offer lasting peace and satisfaction. If you place your trust in them they will eventually disappoint or destroy you. The Lord told Judah to stop trusting in people and the works of their hands. Isa.2:22, Stop trusting in man who has but a breath in his nostrils. Of what account is he? Human or mortals and things are temporary. God is immortal, permanent, eternally, trust worthy and strong. He's a safe Haven for His people to trust in good times and bad times. Ps.146:5-10, Do not put your trust in princes or in mortal man who cannot save you. Blessed is he whose help is in the God of Judah. The maker of Heaven, earth, sea and everything in them, the Lord who remains faithful forever. He upholds the cause of the oppressed and gives food to the hungry. The Lord gives sight to the blind, the Lord lift up those who are bowed down, the Lord loves the righteous. The Lord watches over the alien or strangers and sustains the fatherless and the widow. The Lord reigns forever, your God O Zion for all generations. Praise the Lord. The Lord God Almighty is the only one whom you can fully trust. Jer.17:7-8, Blessed is the one who trust in the Lord whose confidence is in Him. He will be like a tree planted by the river that sends out roots by the stream. It does not fear and never fails to bear fruit. We Christians are to be like that. We need not to worry when problems or troubles come because He's always with us. He said He'd never leave or forsake His children. When we're going through a valley in our life He is right there with us. He is our strength, our refuge, our salvation and our keeper. The joy of the Lord is our strength. Gal.20:25, We should always bear fruit of joy, peace, love, faithfulness, gentleness,

5

goodness and self control. If we live by the Spirit then we should walk in the Spirit. Believers can enjoy the freedom to participate in the works of the Spirit. As we allow ourselves to be led by the Holy Spirit, evidence of our freedom, the fruit of the Spirit will appear in our lives. We will trust God more. The more we trust him the more we'll serve Him. God can move in every situation, nothing's too big or too small for Him. He cares for you and me. The Bible says to trust no man for they will fail you. Trust God with all your heart, mind, soul and strength.

Fear and worry is sin
Seven fears and worry factors:

1- Fear is the rejection of faith

2- Fear is the proof that you don't trust God in your crises

3- Fear brings worry

4- Worry is a killer

5- Worry robs the body of rest

6- Worry causes a lot of illnesses

7- Worry has no place in the life of a Christian.

There is a righteous fear. Prov.1:7, The fear of the Lord is the beginning of knowledge but fools despise wisdom and instructions. Isa.8:13, Sanctify the Lord of hosts Himself and let Him be your fear and let Him be your dread or worry. Matt. 10:28, Do not fear those that can kill the body but fear Him that can destroy the body and soul in hell. Only God can do that. He's the One who you must fear. Fear in this case is love. But you need to fear what will happen to you if you don't serve and follow Him. God is love but He's also a God of judgment as well. We are to fear God and honor Jesus Christ. Luke 1:50, His mercy is on them that fear Him from generation to generation. God is saying from beginning to the end. God's mercy endures forever. It's because of His mercy and grace that is laid up for all that love and fear Him. Just like a father pities his children when they do wrong so does our Heavenly Father pities His children. The Lord takes pleasure in those who fear and have hope in His mercy. Fear in the Lord is the right way and the right fear. Fear in the Lord is to love and trust Him in everything. Fear is the beginning of wisdom as well as understanding. Prov.3:7, Be wise in your own eyes, fear the Lord and depart from evil. Even when you lie down you will not be afraid. We should never be afraid of sudden fear. Prov.8:13, The fear of the Lord is to hate evil, pride, arrogance and the evil way of the forward mouth. God said He hated a forward mouth. This is what you call a big mouth. One who talks too much, loud and boisterous. They know how and can control everything else but no one can tame the tongue for it's like burning fire. Proverbs talks a lot about fear. It tells us that the fear of the Lord prolongs days of our lives. They that walk in His righteousness fears the Lord. A wise person fears and departs from evil. The fear of the Lord is strong confidence and His children shall have a place of refuge. The fear of the Lord is a fountain of life to depart from the snares of death. It's better to have little with fear of the Lord than great treasures and troubles there with. The fear of the Lord is the instruction of wisdom and before honor is humility. The fear of the Lord tends to life and they that have it shall be satisfied and they shall not be visited with evil. By humility and fear of the Lord are riches, honor and life. We should never envy sinners for what they have but have fear of the Lord all the days of our lives. Ecc.12:13, Let us hear the conclusion of the whole matter. Fear God and keep His commandments for this is the whole duty of man. Serve the Lord with fear and rejoice in trembling. The fear of the Lord is clean, enduring forever. When you fear the Lord also praise and worship Him in the beauty of holiness. When we fear the Lord He will show us the way He will teach us in the way that He has planned for us. Ps.46:1, God is our refuge and Strength, a very present help in time of trouble. This is one of my favorite scriptures. Just think, He is right there with you even before troubles starts. He is present, right there with us and He's our strength and refuge our safe place in times of trouble and sorrows. Prov.29:25, The fear of man brings a snare or a net, but whoever puts their trust in the Lord shall be safe. Here is a warning for those who fear things and worry about things. We have to be careful what we say and what we think as well. The devil starts in the mind trying to put things there to hinder Christians and cause fear and worries. Prov.10:24, What the wicked dread will come upon them but what the righteous desire shall be granted. We need to desire the things of the Lord and not be among the wicked that worry and fear. God wants us to be free from all worries. We need to cast all of our cares upon Him for He cares for us. What can you add to your life by worrying? My dad always said, worry will not change a thing, it will only make a problem worse. Phil.4:6, Be anxious in nothing but in everything in prayer and supplication with thanksgiving and let your request be known to God. Why do you worry? It won't change a thing, for it will make things worse. It causes more problems. A person can worry until they are sick in body. Some people worry to the extent that they take their own life because they can't take it or cope anymore. That's why the Word tells us to trust God in all things and He will work it all out for us. If we love Him then we will trust Him and He will bring it to pass. There are many things too big for us to handle in this life ourselves. God said He would make a way where there seem to be none. He told us to bring all of our burdens to Him. When we are weak then we are strong in Him. God has not given us the spirit of fear but of power, love and a sound mind. When you worry or fret it hard to have a sound mind or even show love at times and we have no power because we try to do things our way and not God's way. Doubt and worry are the opposite of faith. When we doubt we receive nothing from the Lord. James tells us that if we doubt we receive nothing. We have to ask in faith, believing that it's going to come to pass whatever we ask. A person who wavers will receive nothing says James. Faith is the substance of things hoped for but not seen. If you see something then you don't have to have faith to believe it. Don't let the sin of worry and fear be in your temple. Your body is the temple of the Lord and we are to take care of it and keep it holy unto the Lord. God will take care of His children, so trust him, love Him, be obedient to Him and let Him lead and guide you all the way. He wants all of you not just a part of you. If you say you trust him and then worry then you really don't trust Him at all. Some can trust Him in little things but not in big things. There's nothing too big for God to handle. Just think how much better you'd be if you will just put it all in His hands and let Him work it all out.

Chapter 2

You cannot serve two masters

*W*e have to choose today whom we will serve. You are either for Christ or you are against Him. There is no in between when it comes to serving the Lord. You can fool a lot of people but you will never fool God for He sees everything and He knows the heart. He knows the intentions of your heart. People look on the outside but God judges the heart. If the heart is pure then the rest of the body is clean.

Matt. 6:24, No one can serve two masters for he will hate the one and love the other or he will be devoted to one and despise the other. You cannot serve God and mammon, which is money or anything that you put before God. Lots of people worship their money and what it can buy for them or what it can do for them. You have to have money to survive but that's not happiness that's lasting. It may bring you some happiness for a while but it's not completely fulfilling. Only the Master, Jesus Christ can do all of these things. You can't take your money with you when you leave this world. You brought nothing into this world and you will carry nothing out of this world with you. All you will take with you is what you have done and accept Jesus as your Lord and Savior and then follow Him until the end. He that endures to the end the same shall be saved. Matt.6; 19-21, Do not store up for yourselves treasures on earth where moth and rust destroy and thieves break in and steal. But store up in Heaven where they will not be destroyed and where thieves do not break in and steal. For where your treasure is there your heart will be also. Prov.23:4, Do not wear yourself out to be rich, have wisdom to show restraints. The love of money is the root of all money. Money is not a sin but the love of it is.

Lots of rich people are the most unhappiest people in the world. Many become greedy and proud when they become rich. They look down at others because they don't measure up to them. They become so involved in what they have done with their money that they miss out on the most precious things. They don't have time for their family and the most precious things in life. They don't feel they need God for they have their money. It becomes a god to them. Not all rich are like that but if you took inventory you would find many in this category. James 5:1-6, Listen you rich people, weep and mourn riches are corroded, it will testify against you for you have hoarded up wealth in the last days. You have failed to pay your workers their wages. You have lived on earth in luxury and self indulgence, you have made yourself fat and wanted nothing. You have condemned and murdered innocent people who were not opposing you. He is saying here, you have allowed many people to starve to death and you wouldn't help them. You might be saying, it wasn't my duty to feed the hungry or clothe the needy. Whatever we do it's like doing it to Christ. Jesus said what you do for others you do for Me. All these sayings of Jesus are for the Christian. So, you Christians who are rich have these commands of Jesus Christ. We are our brothers and sisters keeper. If they are hungry we are to feed them and if they need clothing we are to see that they are clothed. We are to take care of the widows and the fatherless and orphans. Many churches are neglecting their duty in this area. Look at verse 3 again. You have hoarded up wealth in the last days. Many will preach and teach that Jesus is coming soon but they still are making long time plans here on this earth. It's nothing wrong to have a little nest egg for a rainy day I believe, but God said not to hoard it up. Many churches are large with many rooms and space but they would never allow to take the homeless in, feed them and give them a warm place to stay until they can do better. God is not pleased with this. The preachers preach to give but how much do they give? It seems the small churches do the most giving with the experiences my husband and I have experienced in traveling and ministering.

Luke 12:33-34, Jesus taught them to sell all of their possessions and give to the poor, provide purses for yourselves that will not wear out. A treasure in Heaven is the purse He was talking about. That is the only kind of purse that will last forever. For where your treasure is there will your heart be also. Jesus said, a rich man will hardly enter into the Kingdom of Heaven. We are to help the needy, the lowly and all who are in need. Matt.26:31-46, The scripture tells us what to do. Anything we do for others we do for Christ.

We will be judged on the basic of our response to human needs. Whatever is offered to the least of these is offered to Him. No gift is unimportant. A cup of water given in Jesus name, a coat, a visit to the prison or hospital and other good deeds. The rich fall into many temptations and snares and many foolish and hurtful lusts lead to destruction. Ask yourself this question, is money important enough to keep you from going to Heaven?

I Cor.6; 9, Those who love God are known by Him. The Lord is good and He knows them that trust Him. He knows His sheep by name. John 10:3, I am the good Shepherd and I know My sheep and I am known by mine. The Lord knows them that are His. It's so exciting to know that Jesus knows my name. He said I am His and He is mine. The foundation of God stands strong, it stands sure. II Tim. 2:19, Let everyone that name the name of the Jesus Christ depart from iniquity, sin. Depart form the love of money and other gods in your life. Whatever you spent the most time in becomes your god. God said, there shall be no other god before Me. You shall love the Lord with all your heart, with all your soul, with all your mind and with all your strength. Then you shall love your neighbor as yourself. How much do you love yourself? You can measure how much you love yourself by the way you love your neighbor is really what God is saying. Acts 20:35, I have shown you all of these things, how you should support the weak and to remember the Words of the Lord Jesus Christ. It is more blessed to give than to receive. Rom.15:5, We who are strong ought to bear the infirmities of the weak and not to please ourselves. We are to bear one another's burdens and fulfill the law of Christ. We are to show kindness, mercy, humbleness of mind, meekness and long suffering. We are to forbear one another and forgive each other. We are to bear with the hurting, the lonely and the needy. Above all, put on love which is the bond of perfection, have the peace of God and do His will. It's not all about us and doing what we want but what He wants. Reach out to someone and the greatest joy and peace will come over you. Try it for it's a great experience. It's so much better to give than to receive. Whatever you do in word or deed do it all in the name of the Lord Jesus Christ giving thanks to God the Father by Him. Heb. 13:3, Remember them that are in bonds as bound with them which suffer adversity as being there yourself. We are to all be of one mind having compassion on one another, love the brethren, be pitiful, have sympathy for others and be courteous. We are to render out blessings knowing that we will then receive blessings. People say you don't give to get back and you don't. But Jesus said, When you give you shall receive so we can expect something back because He said it. Prov28:20, A faithful man shall abound with blessings. James 1:27, Pure religion and undefiled before God and the Father is this, to visit the widows and the fatherless in their afflictions and to keep yourselves unspotted from the world.

God's blessings and riches

God has many blessings for His children, to those who are faithful and true to Him. Many miss out on His blessings because they are not obedient and faithful to Him. God has so many benefits for His children and it's not His fault if you miss out on these blessings. You have to do something to receive. There are always requirement for blessings. You can't just sit back and think that God will just drop them into your lap. Prov.10:22, The blessings of the Lord makes rich and He adds no sorrow with it. There are many who make themselves rich but have nothing. Then there are those that make themselves poor yet have great riches. It is a sure thing that we brought nothing into this world and we can carry nothing out. Where will your riches be when you are gone from this world? Rev.3:17-18, Because you say, I am rich and increased in goods and have need of nothing and know not that you are wretched, miserable, poor, blinded and naked. Buy of Me gold tried in the fire so you may be rich and wear clothes so you won't be ashamed and naked, anoint your eyes with salve so you can see. Luke 12: 20-21, Your soul shall be required of you, so is he that lay up treasures for himself and not rich toward God.

Where is you treasure? What is your treasure? Where is your heart? Who is your master? Who are you serving? Remember, true Christianity is taking care of the needy, lonely, sick, those in prisons, anyone who is hungry and thirsty, the ones out in the cold and the poor. It is our Christian duty all that are called by the name of Jesus Christ to do our part and obey His commands in everything He said. Lets be faithful to Him above all others and other things so He will be pleased with us and will one day say to us, Well done My faithful ones for you and proven Me and seen that Iwill do what I said. He will never fail you and me so we should never fail Him either. He wants to bless His children but we must bless others. Give and it shall be given unto you, pressed down and running over. In Malachi the Scripture tells us that when we give our tithe and offering we will receive a blessing that we won't even have room to contain it. Can you imagine not having room enough to store our blessings? Have you tried

God and let Him prove to you what He will do? He's got all you need and then more. Serve God and Him only and reap the benefits here and now and then eternal life to come. God is good.

You can have confidence in God to do what He said

We have to reverence Him, obey, honor and love Him above all others and everything else in our lives. He has to be first place above all else and all others. He said to keep His commandments, serve Him and do His work. We have to be His hands, feet and mouth and to be long suffering toward others and show mercy. We have to walk in His footsteps. He that gives mercy shall receive mercy. Be careful where your feet take you and what comes out of your mouth. Let wisdom and understanding lead you, for true wisdom is of God.

Ps.27:13-14, I am still confident of this, I will see the goodness of the Lord in the land of living. David is saying, I know I will make it through this life to see the Promised Land. I will be in Heaven the land of living. He was assured of what God had said He would do, if he continued to love and trust Him always and endure to the end. David said, wait on the Lord with patience and be strong. Just because you don't see anything happen right away when you pray and ask God for something, don't give up, wait upon the Lord for the answer is coming. Ps.40:1, David said, I waited patiently for the Lord. He turned to me and answered my prayer. Now if God answered right away then David wouldn't have had to wait patiently, would he? Many times God says wait when we ask for something. Maybe He wants to see if we are going to wait with patience or maybe it's not good for us to have what we have asked for right away. Sometimes it good for us to wait. We are such a spoiled people that we want what we want right now. We can't tell God when to give to us what we ask for, for God knows best for us. We fail to ask His will to be done in our lives, many times. There are times when we will receive right away, sometimes He says no, but sometimes He says to wait with patience. God is trying to teach us to wait with patience and with confidence in Him knowing that He is in control and will do the best for His children. If we will meditate on these words that David has said, we can give thanks to God for His wisdom toward us. When we place out confidence in God we will never be dissatisfied. Just wait with confidence in God knowing we will see the goodness of the Lord.

Ps.29:11, The Lord gives strength to His people and blesses them with peace. Our peace comes from God for within us there is no peace. Praise be to Him forever for the peace He gives unto us. David said, I wait for the Lord, my soul waits and in His Word I put my hope. My soul waits for the Lord more than watchmen wait for morning. Isaiah 32:17, The affect of righteousness will be confidence forever. If we live righteous and holy in the Lord we can be confident always that God will do what He says. If you are not one of His and you're not living a holy life then you can't expect for God to even hear your prayers much less answer them. He says He turns His face from sin and will not even hear when you pray. You can find that in Isaiah. The prayers of the righteous prevail much. Many times someone is praying for you that are in the Lord and God will move on their behalf. That's why God says for us to stand in the gap for others. I thank God for a dear uncle, a saint of God, who was praying for me when I wasn't living the way I should. He kept lifting me up to God and I praise God for Him. He's gone on to be with the Lord now but I will always be thankful to him and praise God for him for standing in the gap for me.Ps.3:6, For the Lord will be your confidence and keep you from being snared. God will take care of His children who follow Him daily. He said to pick up your cross and follow Him daily. Blessed are the ones who trust in the Lord whose confidence is in Him. Phil.3:3, We are the circumcision who worship God in the Spirit and rejoice in the Lord Jesus Christ and have no confidence in the flesh but in Him.

Heb.3:14, We have come to share Christ if we hold firmly to the end in the confidence we had at first. We have to hold on, never give up or give in to the devil's snares. The devil is always going to be around to try to cause you all the problems he can but you have to flee from him. That's his job and he does it well. We have to hold on tightly to the things of God. Stay in His Word and in His will and resist the devil. Heb.4:16, Let us then approach the throne of grace with confidence so that we may receive mercy and find grace to help us through the times of need. We have this confidence to enter the most high place by the blood of Jesus, Verse 35, don't throw your confidence away for it will be richly rewarded. Believe what you ask and it will come to pass. It may not be when you want it but it will come according to God's will and not yours. God is always on time and He never makes a mistake. You can stand on the Word of God. I John 5:14-15, this is the confidence that we have approaching God, that if we ask anything according to His will He hears us. We have to know that

He hears us, we have to believe and not doubt. Have you ever prayed and then wondered if God heard you? John said we have to know that He hears us. Just pray and leave it in His hands. We can put our trust in the Lord both now and forever for He never changes. His love is unfailing and with Him is full redemption. We are redeemed by the blood of Jesus Christ. He died for all but not all accepts it. When you come to Christ then you are not your own, for you were bought with a price. Jesus paid for you with His own blood when He died on the cross at Calvary. Ps.132:1-2, David said, my heart is not proud oh Lord, my eyes are not haughty or arrogant, I do not concern myself with great matters too wonderful or high for me. I have stilled myself as a child that is weaned from its mother, my soul is as a weaned child. He is saying here that he has weaned himself from the flesh doing what he wants to do and leaning on the Spirit of God. He died to himself and trusting God completely. We have to place our childlike trust in God who is always there for us. Amen

How can we know God's will for us?

Prov.13:10, Wisdom is found in those who take advice. If you can't take advice or correction then you have no wisdom. For God chastises those that He loves and we have to listen to Him in order to know and to do His will. I desire to do your will O Lord, David said. Your law is within my heart. First, we have to want God and desire His will to be done in us. Ps.143:10, Teach me to do your will O Lord for You are my God, may Your good Spirit lead me on level ground.

Second, we have to allow Him to teach us His will for our lives. We have to listen to Him and be obedient to Him in all things. We can't do things on our own anymore, because when we lean on self then we aren't leaning on Him. We messed up enough before we came to Jesus so now we need to trust and lean on Him for everything.

Thirdly, We have to choose to do God's will, and then we will know it comes from Him. Acts 20:27, For I have not hesitated to proclaim to you the will of God. Paul is saying, I have told you how to live in God's will. Obey His commandments, trust Him and serve Him all the days of your life. There is no excuse for not knowing how to live godly and stay in God's will for it's been well proclaimed in the Word of God. Verse 35,

I have shown you all things, how to labor to support the weak and to remember the Words of the Lord Jesus how He said, It's more blessed to give than to receive. There's so much in the Word of God to show us how to live in His will.

Fourthly, we have to proclaim and accept the will of God for our lives. Rom12:12, Do not be conformed to this world but be ye transformed by the renewing of your mind, then you will know what God's will is. Be not as the world you live in and don't do the things of this world. We have to be different, we have to separate ourselves from the world, from all of the evil and wickedness. God is our father and we have to follow Him. The devil is the father of the world and all of the evil and wickedness.

Fifthly, do not be of this world. We are in this world but we are not of it if we belong to Christ. We are to renew our minds daily and live after God's ways and live holy, without sin. If you do sin you have an Advocate to the Father, Jesus Christ who will intercede for you and He will forgive you. You can't live holy with sin in your life. We are to be reconciled to God. To be reconciled means to be satisfied. Rejoice in Him for His saving grace, love and mercy toward you. Don't be foolish but learn the will of God for your life.

Sixth, it is highly important to know the will of God for our lives. Phil.2; 13, For it is God that works in you to will and act according to His purpose. We need always to pray that God will have His will in our life. We have to be willing for His will to be done.

I can remember in 2002 when my husband was so ill with Hairy Cell Leukemia. His spleen was so full of cancer and had poisoned his entire body. The Dr. told us that he wouldn't live two days without the surgery, to remove these two organs and that if he was operated on, that he wouldn't come off of the operating table alive. My husband told them that they couldn't tell when he was going to die. He told the Dr. to do what he could and that God would do the rest. I was holding on by faith that God was going to heal him and I wouldn't doubt. My husband looked at me the night before surgery and said to me, honey you have to let God have His way. That was really the only way I allowed fear to come into my heart. He said, you have to pray and ask God to have His way. I said, I can't because it may not be God's will for you to live and I have prayed and believed that you are going to be healed and well again. I couldn't bear the thought of him being gone and I'm still here. I laid there in the bed with him in the hospital room and we prayed together and I still couldn't pray for God to have His way and will to be done. Time passed by and I finally prayed, God you have always taken care of us and blessed us so abundantly so now again I ask You to have Your will be done. I had such a peace within that I got up and asked my two daughters to make me some coffee. They said, it's 2:30 in the morning. I said, I know. I knew God had it all in control, He did all of the time but He wants us to tell Him that we trust Him in all things, even when near death. Everyone was expecting him not to make it but I never felt that way. God had given me such peace there was no room for doubt or worry. Only God can do that. He said that He would give us peace that passes all other understanding. I held on the Words of God, I shall live and not die and do the works of the Lord. That was nine years ago and he's still with me, praise the Lord.

Seventh, it is God that works in us and shows us His will for us. Thessalonians 4:3, It is God's will that you be sanctified. We have to live a holy life acceptable unto Him. We have to live above sin. We cannot have sin in our lives because God does not look upon sin for sin separates you from God. We are to rejoice evermore and pray without ceasing, in everything give thanks for this is the will of God in Christ Jesus concerning you and me. Quench not the Spirit, despise not prophesying. Prove all things and hold fast to what is good. Abstain from all appearances of evil. This is what Paul said, stay away from all sin. Keep your eyes, ears, feet, hands and lips from all sin. Don't let temptations cause you to yield and fall away from God. We are living in the last days as we know it here on this earth so keep yourselves in the Lord. Even in bad times we should be thankful to God because He told us we'd have troubles and trials but rejoice for He will deliver us out of them all and make a way for all of His children.

Heb.10:7, Jesus said, here I am, I have come to do Your will O God. To be like Jesus we have to say, I am here to do Your will O Father. Jesus prayed to the Father before He went to the cross. God, if it be Your will let this cup pass from Me. Many times in our lives we may not want to do certain things or go certain places but we have to pray as Jesus prayed to the Father. Lord, Your will be done and not mine. God never said that it would be easy serving Him but it was rewarding. James 4:15, We ought to say, if it be Thy will, we will live and do this or that. We should never want to do or go anyplace if it's not God's will for us. We need to always seek Him and His will for us. We will be happier in the long run. We should never walk ahead of God, or walk behind Him. We want Him to walk right beside us all of the way. I John 5:14, If we ask anything according to His will He hears us and He will answer us either right away, tell us to wait or He will just say no. Whatever the answer might be we have to trust Him and leave it all in His hands for He knows best for His children. Don't question God, just trust and obey him.

Remember, you can't serve two masters. You have to choose which you will serve. There are only two ways to choose. God's way or the devil's way. Everyone has to make that choice for themselves. Just because your father and mother, sisters and brothers belong to God doesn't mean that you automatically become one of God's children. You have a free will, a choice for God doesn't make anyone serve him. God's way means eternal life in the Kingdom of God. The devil's way means death and destruction and your final place will be in hell with all of the sinners and those who denied Jesus Christ as their Savior. This life is but a short one so you have to make your plans here for the next one. When you choose to serve God there is a wonderful life to come. There will be no more pain, sorrow, sickness, death or any kind of problems. Heaven is going to be a beautiful place and you don't want to miss it. Jesus will be there and all the saints of God that has gone on before us. Heaven will surely be worth it all. I want to go there, don't you? Start making your plans today to serve the Lord Jesus Christ. Live everyday like it's going to be your last day here. Jesus is coming for His church so be ready. And if you have to go by death you will still be ready if you endure to the end in Christ. Today is the day of salvation. Joshua said, choose you this day whom you will serve but for me and my house we will serve the Lord. This is what my husband, Leon and I have done. We have chosen to serve the Lord with everything within us and with everything we have. We belong to Him and everything that we have belongs to Him. Praise Him forever. Amen

Chapter 3

Keep Yourselves from This Evil Generation

There are many warning about this subject in the Word of God. This is an evil generation that we're living in today. It has been so for many years now but has gotten much worse. It seems to get worse as the time goes on. Of course, this has been predicted by the prophets of old. There seem to be sin on every corner and everywhere you look. The main thing for you and me is not to get involved in any of this evil going on. All evil and wickedness comes from our enemy, the devil.

Acts 2:40-41, With many words Peter exhorted, warned and pleaded all to save themselves from this corrupt generation. Those that gladly received his words were baptized and the same day there were added unto them about three thousand. Jesus Christ called them a perverse and faithless generation. That sounds like the time we're living in today. There are so many that does not want to hear the Word of God. Many hear it but don't want to obey it. As we study we will see that we need to stay away from the evil around us. It seems all respect is gone from this generation we live in today. Young people and older ones alike want to do their thing. There are no morals, no respect for themselves or others either.

Luke 9:41, Jesus said unto them, you faithless and perverse generation, how long shall I be with you and suffer? He was saying, how long do I have to put up with you? His disciples were powerless. If Jesus was that disgusted with His chosen disciples, how much more do you think that He's disgusted with the sinners and those in this generation that won't serve Him and heed to His Words? Many Christians today have a very little

19

faith. Lot of the churches doesn't even teach on faith and how important it is. Without faith you are dead, the same is without works. Faith without works is dead. They both go hand in hand. Faith is believing something that you can't see and have never seen. To make Heaven you have to have faith in Jesus Christ because you have never seen Him.

Matt. 12:39-40, An evil and perverse generation seeks after a sign and there shall be no sign given but the sign of the prophet Jonah. Jesus was saying, you're looking for proof but you're looking for the wrong kind. All you want is something to satisfy your curiosity, to satisfy your lust of miracles. The only proof you're going to get is what looks like the absence of proof, Jonah's evidence. Jonah was in the belly of a whale for three days and three nights just like the Son of man was in the heart of the earth for three days and nights. This was a true sign, believe it. When Jonah preached to them they changed their lives. Now a far better preacher is here, Jesus Christ and you still seek about proof. We don't need proof for we have the truth. All we have to do is believe it and follow Him. Don't be in the group of this faithless and perverse generation. The just shall live by faith. For without faith you cannot please God the Father.

Matt.3:7-8, John rebuked the Pharisees and the Sadducees and said, O generation of vipers who has warned you to flee from the wrath to come. He called them snakes. They were coming to be baptized because it was a popular thing to do. John was saying, do you think a little water or your snake skins will make a difference? You must repent and bring forth good fruits. It's your life that's got to change not just your skin. You do the changing first and then you get baptized. Being baptized doesn't change a thing in your life without repentance. You must accept the Lord Jesus Christ in your heart and life and become a new person and then be baptized. Baptism is a sign of death, burial and resurrection. Dying to self, bury your old self and rising up a new person in Christ. Baptism is not just formalism but it is the outer sign of the old person going under the water to be cleansed and coming up out of the water a new person in Christ. Now, you can become dirty again if you fail to follow Christ and be faithful and true to Him. So be sure to keep your heart and life clean and holy in Him.

Verse 9, Don't be fooled because you say within yourself that you are a son of Abraham. You can't go to Heaven because of someone else no matter who you belong to. It's an individual decision for each one to choose the right way. What counts in your life? Are you bearing good fruits? Is it green and blossoming? If it is dead wood then it will be cut down and thrown into the fire and burned. Just because your parents are saved and on the way to Heaven, don't mean that you are. You have to choose for yourself whom you will serve. The only way to escape this perverse and evil generation is to come to the Lord Jesus Christ and live for Him. Repent of your sins and serve Him with all of you heart, mind, soul and strength.

Prov.30:12, There is a generation that are pure in their own eyes and yet is not washed from their filthiness. They feel they can live any ole way, do whatever feels good and make it into the Kingdom of Heaven. Not so! Some say, I believe in God and I pray everyday, all of the time. But the devil believes and trembles because he knows where he's going. If you read and study God's Word, the Bible, then you know where you are going too. Knowing about God is not enough. You must have a relationship with Him. You must be obedient and faithful to Him at all times. You have to give Him your whole life not just part of it. Without Jesus in your life you cannot keep yourself from this evil and perverse generation and make it into the Kingdom of Heaven. Don't be fooled by the devil. Prov.12:15, The way of a fool is right in his own eyes. This is what you call self righteousness. Prov.20:6, Most men will proclaim everyone his own goodness, but a faithful man who can find? Outside of Jesus Christ there is none good. You are nothing without Him. You can do nothing without Him whether you believe it or not. Without Him you would not move or breathe. You would not have any strength without Him. We have no righteousness without God being in us. You may think that you have no sin and you do nothing wrong. But if you don't have Jesus Christ in your heart and life and you're not serving Him then you have committed the biggest sin of all. That's rejecting Jesus as your Lord and Savior and you belong to this evil and perverse and adulterous generation. John 3:16, He that believes on the Lord Jesus Christ has everlasting life but he that believes not shall not see life but the wrath of God abides in him.

John 8::24, I said unto you that you shall die in your sins for you believe not that I am He. If you die in your sins and never confess Christ as your Lord and Savior then you will die the second death and be judged and cast into the lake of fire along with the devil and his followers. If you accept Christ as your Savior, then when you die you will be raised up from the grave at rapture of the church and your body will be changed into a body like Jesus Christ and live forever. Why would anyone want to miss Heaven? Your life here as a follower of Jesus is a much sweeter one, much happier one and much more rewarding. You have life more abundantly in Jesus. He gets sweeter as the days go by. Someone said, and I quote, I would rather live my life as if there is a God and die to find out there isn't, than to live my life as if there isn't and die to find out there is. It's going to be a bad thing when people stand before God in the judgment and have to hear Jesus say to them, Sorry. I never knew you, depart from Me you worker of iniquity and then be cast into the lake of fire where the fire is never quenched. This is not a fable it is the truth, the Word of God. I wish I could make everyone believe this. I can't even imagine how bad this would be.

Perverseness is a breach, a violation in the spirit of man. Prov.12:8, They that has a perverse heart shall be destroyed. Prov.28:6, Better is the man that is poor and walks uprightly then he that is perverse in his ways though he be rich. People that have a perverse mind think that gain is godliness from such withdraw yourself. (I Tim.6:5) Perverseness is of the devil, he causes the mind to think things in a different way and it's always the wrong way. The devil can cause the minds of people to be robbed of the truth. Watch out for these leaders that use God and His ministry for self gain in money and things of this world. They think that because of the self gain that they have it because they live so godly. This makes them a perverse and adulterous person in our generation. The only way we can truly gain is spiritually, and it has to be God's way, all the way forever. I don't believe that God is pleased when you have to get on TV or any where and beg for money. Jesus walked everywhere He went to preach the gospel. Why do so many preachers have to have their own airplane to travel where they want to and boast about how they are debt free. Why don't they help other to be debt free if they have so much? Lord help us in the perverse and evil generation. Jesus rebuked the doubters and perverse generation when He said, O faithless and perverse generation. Jesus said, humble yourself as a little child, be born again as a little child and come follow Me. He said, take up your cross and follow Me.

God warns about stubbornness and rebellion

The Lord told Moses that the people are a stiffed neck people. The Israelites refused to obey the man of God, Samuel. They would not obey the king Saul because they wanted to be worldly like all of the other nations. Like the people today in whom we live, they listen to everyone else but the men and women of God. They want to be like the world and do their own thing and do it their way for they are stubborn and rebellious. II Chr.24:19, The Lord sent prophets to them and they testified against them and they would not listen. Just like today, God has sent Spiritual men and women, prophets and they have taught them and warned the people but they won't listen. They are stiffed neck, evil and rebellious people. Jeremiah said, they have turned their backs to me and not their faces even though I have taught them. They have not hearkened to me to receive good instructions. They have rejected God and His truth and His ways. They have even polluted the house of God. They did abominations in the temple of God. We see this today in our churches. They bring things into the house of God that is worldly and God is not pleased with that. God's house is a holy place and we should keep it that way. It's a place of worship to the only holy and True God. You remember when Jesus went into the temple and they were buying and selling there in the temple, He over threw the money changers and put them out and said to them. My house is a house of worship but you have made it a den of thieves. Jesus was angry when He did this. I believe He is angry with the churches today that allow these things to go on in the house of God for it should be kept holy unto God.

Zec.7; 11, They refused to listen and they pulled away and shrugged their shoulders and shut up their ears so they couldn't hear. They were spiritually deaf and despised the Word of God. Their hearts were hardened, they were stubborn and evil. We see this still today in many people and many places. They want to go their way and do their own thing. Paul said, you stiffed neck and uncircumcised in heart and ears. You always resist the Holy Spirit as your fathers did. You have sinned against the Holy Spirit. We do have a lot of influence on our children so we need to always be careful what we say and how we live. Our testimonies are not only for our children but for the world. According to the Bible there has been rebellious people over all of the generations because the Israelites were rebellious and then Jesus said there were rebellious people when He walked the earth and then Paul talked about the rebellious people in his time. We know there are rebellious people today everywhere on the earth. I believe that it's much worse now than then.

The danger of not listening

God turns a deaf ear to those who are living in sin. He said that He would not look upon sin. He said also that He didn't hear or answer a sinner's prayer. If He turned His face away for a moment, from His only begotten Son, Jesus Christ when He took all of the world's sin upon His back, why wouldn't He turn His back on sin today? Zech.7:12-13, There came a great wrath from the Lord of hosts. As the Lord cried out unto them they would not hear. So when they cried out unto the Lord He would not hear them either. Their prayers were not heard and not answered. God does not hear a sinner's prayer. The only prayer He hears from a sinner is when they come to Him with a sorrowful heart because of sin and want to repent. God will cast them away because they did not hearken to Him, talking about the Israelites here. But it stands the same today for God never changes, He's the same yesterday, today and forever. God's Spirit will not always strive with man. Today is the day of salvation so come to Him and accept Him in your heart and life while there is time for one day it will be too late.

We are to warn people of their evil ways and if they do not turn from them then they will die in their sins. The blood won't be on our hands if we tell them and they refuse to listen. We are to encourage them not to sin and about their unruly and evil ways. We are to continue to warn people of their sins and wrong ways until Jesus come or as long as we live here on this earth. We are to encourage them to follow Christ and turn from this evil and perverse generation.

Rev.21:8, Tells where the sinners will end up for eternally, the fearful, unbelieving, abominable, murderers, and brimstones, which is the second death. You don't want to go there. The only way to escape hell is to accept Jesus Christ as your Lord and Savior and Master of your life with all of your heart, soul, mind and strength. Accept Him today for tomorrow may be too late.

Be sure your sins find you out

Rom.1:18, For the wrath of God is revealed from Heaven against all ungodliness and unrighteousness of men who hold the truth in righteousness. God's anger rises as the acts of human mankind sin and mistrust Him. People try to put a shield over sin. God says to make sure your sins find you out. Just confessing Him with your mouth is not enough. The Word of God has given us all of the directions we need to follow Him and live godly and holy lives before Him in this present world. You can't live as the world lives and still be a Christian and please God at the same time. You have to be different from the world to be His children. Come out from them God tells us. We can't go where the world goes or talk like the world talks or do what they do.

Rom.6:12-15, Let not sin reign in your mortal bodies and obey it in the lust thereof. Neither yield your members or instruments unto unrighteousness and sin but yield yourselves unto God as those that are alive from the dead and your instruments of righteousness unto God. Remember, when you were first saved and you invited Jesus in your heart and life and you repented of your sins? He forgave you so you were actually raised from the dead and now you live in Him for you have become a new person in Christ Jesus. We don't live under the law now for we live under grace and faith in Jesus Christ. God forbid that you sin or do as the world. Don't give sin the time of the day and don't let sin tempt you in doing anything that's not of God. Don't even run a little errand that connects with your old life you once lived. Serve God full time with your whole heart, soul, mind and strength. You're lot living the devil's way now for you are living God's way, in holiness and righteousness. Verse 23, For the wages of sin is death.

II Kings 22:13, For great is the wrath of God that is kindled against us because of not hearkening to the Words of this book, the Bible and not doing what is written thereof. We are to read and study this book and heed to what it says. The wrath of God is revealed from Heaven against all unrighteousness and ungodly people who hold the truth in righteousness. God hates all sin. There is no little or big sin for sin is sin in God's eyes. Some sin carry a greater penalty. Don't ever think that you're going to get by with sin without paying a penalty. There is a sin of stubbornness, which is witchcraft and that's of the devil. Many don't see this is a sin but God sees it and He calls it sin. The sin of murder stands out to everyone and it is a bad sin but God sees sin as sin. Don't ever think that you are without sin of some kind because John tells us that if we say that we have no sin then we lie and the truth is not in us. Now, we can live above sin but we make mistakes because we are still in this flesh but we are to strive to be perfect just as Jesus is perfect. There are rewards for faithfulness and obedience to God but there is also judgment and fire for the disobedience and rebellion

Chapter 4

Truth Causes Division

*W*hen you come to Jesus Christ you can expect division to enter into your life because Jesus had told us this. When Jesus Christ came in Luke 12:51, Jesus said do you suppose that I have come to bring peace on earth? No I say to you, but rather division. Jesus knew when one accepted Him that it would cause division among family, friends and whoever did not believe in Him. Verse 49 says this, I have come to cast fire upon the earth and how I wish that it was already started. He is saying, I want My people to get on fire for Me. I want to clean up the world He was saying. When you come to Jesus you have to be different from the world because we have to separation ourselves from the world.

Mark 13:12-13, Brothers shall betray brothers to death, fathers the son, children shall rise up against their parents and shall have them put to death. You shall be hated of all people for My name sake but, they that endure to the end the same shall be saved. All people shall hate you because of Me, Jesus is saying. Even back in Isaiah 66:5 the prophet said, hear the Word of the Lord, you who tremble or fear at My Word, your brothers shall hate you and exclude you because of My name. You will be hated by all nations because of Me. Sometimes people will miss understand us, many will dislike us or hate us. Others will go out of their way to cause sufferings and sorrow for us. People are very spiteful, critical, hateful and unloving and kind but just remember, Jesus said it would be this way. Persecutions are never comfortable. The battle is not ours for Jesus has already won the war at Calvary. He made the way, He cleared the way for us to follow.

John 15:18-21, If the world hates you it hated Me first. If you belonged to the world it would love you but, you do not belong to the world and that is why they hate you. If they persecuted Me then you can expect them to persecute you also. They will treat you the way they do because of My name for they do not know Me. Jesus told us not to be surprised if the world hates you. We shouldn't be surprised for the treatment we get from the world because Jesus has already warned His children and His followers what was going to happen. He said don't be alarmed or surprised when you truly stand up for Me. II Tim.3:12 and 14, all that live godly in Christ Jesus will suffer persecutions. He told us to remain faithful to the things we have been taught. Keep on believing and follow Him no matter what. Stay away from anything that would cause you to lust after if it's not of God. Follow the things that make you want to live right, godly and holy. Pursue faith, love, peace and enjoy the companionship of those who call on the Lord with a pure heart. Love your enemies and pray for them, do good to those who mistreat you and say all manner of evil against you for My name sake. Never pay back evil for evil but pay back good for evil. We are to be like Jesus, live like Him and always show forth love to everyone. Jesus Christ is counting on His children to carry out His plans here on earth and we have to do it in love, holiness and faithfulness.

The Bible is our road map here on earth

Read, study, believe it and stand on the Word in all things and be sure to endure to the end. Never sway from the truth of God's Word. It will never lead you in the wrong path. The way is narrow but you still have enough room to travel on this road. There are many curves, bumps and pot holes and trials here on this earth when we follow Jesus but He said He's be with us and make a way where there seem to be none. He is our light so there should never be any darkness on this road for He is the light even in dark times. He has walked down this road before us to He made the way for His children. Jesus said that the way is narrow and few therein will find it. He's talking about the way to Heaven and He is the way, the truth and the light. Jesus has shown us the way so what we need is to follow and go His way. He didn't call us to be liked or loved by everyone. We are to love Him and long for His love for us. We need to long for more of Him.

Jesus never told us that it would be easy following Him but it would be rewarding in the end. From my experience living for Jesus, it's the happiest life you can live. There's no peace in the world but there's peace in Jesus Christ. Even when we go through hard times and troublesome times you can find peace in Him. There's so much hate, so much unbelief, so many trials, so many temptations of family, friends and even church family at times. We have to suffer at times for our faith in God. The prophets and the disciples did and some even died because of their faith in God. Our Lord and Savior Jesus Christ suffered and died a terrible death on the cross for us. He was ridiculed, scoffed at, lie about, spat upon and was tempted of the devil just as we are. He was a real man and walked upon this earth, He lived and died for us and never sinned. So He has paved this road for us to follow and to travel on. Don't lose your road map for it's the road map to Heaven and there's no other way to go except through Jesus Christ for His blood has to wash you to make you clean.

Acts 14:22, Many tribulations we will go through if we follow Jesus and continue in faith. Our light afflictions which is but for a moment works and is achieving for us a far more weight of eternal glory. What we go through here is very small compared to the glory and happiness we'll have in Heaven. It will be worth it all just to see Jesus and then all of the other wonderful things that He has for His children when we get there. We don't have to wait to receive blessing when we get there for He has many blessings here for His children. It's a real blessing to serve Him II Pet.2:9, The Lord knows how to deliver the godly out of temptation and to reserve the unjust on the day of judgment for their punishment.

God called us to be faithful to Him

He has reminded us many times that when persecutions come our way and we stand strong in Him that it evidence that we belong to Him. Stand firm and endure for Jesus said we can because He is with us, He's our strength and our source. II Cor.4:78, We may be troubled on every side but not distressed, perplexed but not in despair, persecuted but not forsaken, cast down but not destroyed. We have problems with all kinds of people in this world, our family, friends, and co-workers and like I said before, sometimes even our church family at times. Luke 6:22, Blessed are you when they shall hate you and when they separate you from their company and shall have a reproach against you and cast out your name as evil for the Son of man's sake. Don't worry when people say evil things about you for they said it about Jesus. Just do unto others as you would have them do unto you. Be patient with people and even to yourself. Luke 21:19, For in your patience you possess your soul, you save and keep it. In the beatitudes we find these promises of God. Blessed are the merciful for they shall obtain mercy. Blessed are the pure in heart for they shall see God. Blessed are the peace makers for they shall be called the children of God. Blessed are you when men shall revile you, persecute you and say all manner of evil against you falsely for My name sake. Jesus said to rejoice and be exceedingly glad when all of this happens to you, for great is your reward in Heaven for so they persecuted the prophets before you.

Promise of the triumph

There's victory in Jesus for over comers. Who shall separate us from the love of Christ? Shall tribulations, distress, persecutions, famine, nakedness, perils or swords? In all these things we are more than conquerors through Him that loves us. We should let nothing or no one come between us and the Lord and what we need to do in His work. Jesus said, I have overcome the world so be of good cheer. He is a good smelling fragrance and He spreads the aroma through His children. II Cor.2: 14-15, Thanks be to God which always causes us to triumph in Christ and makes manifest the savor or taste of His knowledge by us in everyway. For we are to God a sweet favor or taste of Christ in them that are saved. We are the salt of the earth and the light of the world so we should make sure that we live like it all of the time so the unsaved world can see Jesus in us. God is counting on His children, we all have a mission and we need to do it with all of our might. Don't ever think that you're a nobody for you are a child of the King, if you are one of His. Stand strong and firm in the truth and let your faith grow. II Cor.10:4, We are strong and mighty to the pulling down of strong holds through our weapons, prayer, reading and studying God's Word. We're over comers because greater is He that is within us than he that is in the world. Whosoever is born of God over comes the world and this is the victory that over comes the world, even our faith. We can even over come the wicked one, the devil through Jesus Christ.

Rewards of victory

I will keep you from the hour of temptation which will come upon the world. He's talking here about the great tribulation of seven years after the Church has been taken out. He will not leave His church here to go through that bad, bad time. You don't want to be here for that for it will be a time like never before and will never be again. You think things are bad now, you have seen nothing that will compare to that time. Revelation chapters 2 and 3 gives us great promises to the over comers. I will keep you from that time of tribulation. I will give of you to eat of the tree of life. They that overcome I will give to eat the hidden manna and I will give them a white stone with a new name written which no one knows except the one who receives it. They that over comes will I give a white garment and I will not blot their name out of the book of life, I will confess their name before My Father and the angels. Rev. 21:7 They that overcome will inherit all things, I will be their God and they shall be My sons and daughters. Rev.22:14, Blessed are they that do His commandments for they have the right to the tree of life and will enter into the gates of the city. Blessed are they that read, hear and keep His Word. The time is at hand. Are you going to stand with the truth or are you going to be separated from the true and living God? Remember, truth separates, it causes division.

God will bring final division in the end

God will separate the saved from the unsaved in the end. They will be assigned to their final places made for them. It will be Heaven or hell for thee is no in between. Matt.13, Let the tares and wheat grow up together until the time of harvest and I will say to the reapers, gather the tares and bind them in a bundle to burn them, but gather the wheat into the barn. The wheat is being saved. Here we see the Christians are the wheat and the wicked and unsaved are the tares and they will be burned. As therefore the tares are gathered and burned in the fire so shall it be in the end of this age or in this world. The Son of man shall send forth His angels and they shall gather out of His Kingdom all things that offend and them which so iniquity or sin. So shall it be in the end of this age, the angels shall come forth and sever the wicked from among the just. Matt.25:33, And He shall set the sheep on the right side but the goats on the left. The sheep are the saved and the goats are the unsaved. They are divided because the truth separates. Jesus will say to they goats on the left, depart from Me you cursed into everlasting fire prepared for the devil and his angels. These shall go into everlasting punishment.

What is worth more to you today than serving the Lord Jesus Christ? It is better to separate yourself now from the world and serve Him than to wait until you have to be separated by Jesus in the end. You are without excuse because you have heard the truth. The truth shall set you free. The truth shall separate you from the ungodly. In order to gain freedom we have to give freedom. Give of yourself freely to Jesus Christ and He will set you free. He will free you of all of your sins and you will receive the free gift of salvation that only He can give. Live for Him and be an over comer of the world and receive all of the blessings that He has in store for you. Living for Jesus is a good life and it's very rewarding here in this life and then eternal life to come. You will never regret this decision to come to Him. Come as you are and He will clean you up. He will change all of your desires and help you with all of you short comings. He will show you the way. Travel on His road map for it will take you to Heaven. Praise the Lord.

People shall perish because of lack of knowledge

Hosea 4:6, God said, My people shall perish because of the lack of knowledge. This was a charge against Israel but it still stands for us today. The entire book O Hosea gives us a picture of God loving His people in spite of their unfaithfulness. The Israelites were un-stabled and willfully disobedient to God to an all time low. The nations today are in a mess. They're in civil disgust, they're sick, they're rebellious to God all over the world. There's bloodshed everywhere, homes are corrupt, Courts are corrupt, many priests and ministers are even corrupt. There is very little Spiritual health to be found, There's hate all around even in the Christian world.

Hosea 1:2, God chose Hosea to be a prophet and told him to go marry a wife, Gomer his wife was a prostitute. She was unfaithful to Him and had children that were unfaithful. The land was full of adultery and departing from the Lord. God used this marriage illustrate His love for His unworthy, faithless bride, the Israelites. We are the ones that were drafted in so it is still meant for us today. God's children are so unfaithful but He still loves the people but He hates the sins. The people watch Hosea as he stood by his unfaithful wife. He bought her out of slavery and brought her back home with him after all she had done. She surely didn't deserve that kind of love and care from her husband, Hosea. Neither did Israel or we today deserve the love and care that God has given His children. God is love and He loved us enough to send His only begotten Son to die for us. Jesus Christ loved us enough to freely give His life for us. We don't deserve such love. In spite of their godless indifferences, sin seeking and sinning God loved them freely. Hosea pleaded with the people and said, Hear you the Word of the Lord, the Lord has a charge against you. There is no faithfulness, no love, no respect and blood touches blood, meaning, there's killing everywhere. Because of this the land mourns and all who live in it waste away. They will eat but will not have enough, there will be famine in the land. They are unfaithful to the true God. People without understanding will come to ruin. Doesn't this sound like America today?

Does God hide from us? The answer is yes. God says in Hosea 5:6, They will seek the Lord but will not find Him for He has withdrawn Himself from them. It's because of the unfaithfulness He said. I will pour My wrath upon them like a flood of water. When we willfully and consistently disobey Him, He will turn away because He will not look upon sin. He will not abandon anyone if they abide in him. If you stray away and come back to Him He will accept you back. He said, I will not leave you as orphans for I will come to you.

It's a frightening thing to even consider or think about being separated from the love of God even for a moment. We never have to be separated from Him or His love. It's our own choice for He's there to receive us when we come to Him with a sincere heart of repentance and He knows when we are sincere. Are you guilty of Spiritual adultery? He told the Israelite, Your love is like the morning dew. In the early morning dew is there but it goes away soon. This is what you call backsliding or in-stability. Hosea 7, Woe or deep sorrow unto them because they have strayed from Me. Destruction to them because they have transgressed and rebelled against Me. Even though I have redeemed them yet they have spoken lie against Me. They have not cried out to Me with their whole heart. They pretended to come back to Me but they are deceitful and their hearts are hard hearted and faulty. They have turned quickly out of the way that was taught them and walked away in obeying the commandments of the Lord. What they are doing keeps them from coming to the Lord. They are defiled with their own works, the works of the devil. We know our good deeds won't save us or keep us. God wants all of us, our heart, soul, mind and body.

When you truly repent God will accept you back and forgive you. Isa.6:13, Come let us return unto the Lord, He is torn and He will heal us, He has smitten and He will bind us up. When the Israelites sinned and when they truly repented the Lord raised them up and delivered them again, He will do the same for you today. He will bring restoration, Spiritual resurrection and Spiritual life. Isaiah 6:3, Then we will know if we follow on to know the Lord, His coming forth shall come unto us as the rain, as the latter rain into the earth. The latter rain that He will pour upon His children will be the biggest blessing ever. Life eternal with him will be that rain.

God doesn't pay according to our sins

Ps.103:8-13, The Lord is compassionate, gracious, slow to anger and abounding in love. He will not hold His anger forever. He does not treat us as we deserve for we have all sinned and fallen short of the glory of God. If God gave us what we deserved we would all go to hell. We will reap what we sow for the Word tells us this. When God forgives He forgets and doesn't bring it back up to us. He is long suffering, merciful, patience, kind, gentle and His grace endures forever.

But God made a way for us to be able to receive forgiveness through Jesus Christ His Son and have eternal life. If we confess our sins He is faithful and just to forgive and cleanse us from all unrighteousness. We can't earn forgiveness we have to ask for it. If we forgive others then God will forgive us. Jesus didn't die for just a few but He died for all. Praise God for His love, mercy and grace. Thank God that we don't have to pay for our sins in the way they did back in the Old Testament. If they sinned with their hand then their punishment was to cut the hand off. For whatever part of the body they sinned, they paid for their sin. If they were disobedient to their parents they were stoned. Thank God for His grace. We don't live by the law but by grace and by faith in Jesus. Amen

If you go against the grain of wood you will get splinters. Go toward the grain and the wood will be smooth. So if you go against God you will get punished and the wrath of God will come down on you. But if you go His way, trust and obey Him you will be rewarded and have eternal life if you endure to the end in Him. God is a just God and He has no respect of persons. The Bible doesn't say that He is a fair God but a just God. There is a big difference in being fair and being just.

Religion can't save you. Just because your parents took you to church and raise you in church doesn't mean you are saved. Just because you are a Jew doesn't mean you are automatically saved. Just because you are a Catholic you don't get special privileges and you are saved. Don't trust in religion because religion can be a sign of many things. There are many cults, creed and faiths that are called religion. There are atheism, agnosticism and secularism. It's a body of believers worshipping or practicing something on a regular basic. It can be something or someone. People go to work religiously, they eat religiously. Some people go to church every time the doors are opened but that won't save you either. You can't get into the Kingdom of Heaven just by going to church or even being good.

There's a difference in religion and Christianity. To be a Christian you must be saved and the only way to be saved is through Jesus Christ our Lord and Savior. You have to call on Him and invite Him into you heart. You must repent and be sorry for you sins. You then are washed in the blood of Jesus and now you belong to Him. You have to follow Him and be obedient and faithful to Him always. Do we make mistakes? Yes, but we realize it and go to Him and ask forgiveness and He forgives. He doesn't expect us to go and commit the same sin over again and again for we are to learn by our mistakes. For if you continue to sin He will turn your mind over to a reprobate mind like He did to the people in Rome and you will be lost.

Rom.1:28, We will see the danger of sin here. And even as they did not like to retain God in their knowledge, God gave them over to a reprobate mind and to do things which are not convenient. Ignoring God leads to a downward slide. A lot of people know about God but they don't know Him or trust Him as God. They refuse to worship Him or allow Him to lead them in this life. They even confess Him with their mouth but their heart is far from Him because their actions are much different from what they confess. Verse 23, God gave them up to be unclean through the lusts of their own beliefs to dishonor their own bodies. He gave them up to vile affections. There are a lot of lustful sins listed in this chapter. Being filled with unrighteousness, covetousness, maliciousness, full of envy, murder, debate, doubt, deceit, hypocrisy, lies, hateful, tattlers, backbiting, haters of God, pride, inventers of evil things, unmerciful and disobedient to parents.

Without understanding they become foolish and become covenant breakers. They forgot that they had made a covenant with God when they came to Christ. They also break their promises to others. There are immoral sexual desires without natural affection. There are men with men and women with women. God did not make it this way for He made them male and female, husband and wife in Genesis. All kind of unnatural sexual pleasure that is not pleasing to God our Creator. Knowing the judgments of God that they which do such things are worthy of death. Not only the ones who commit these sins but also those who put their approval on those who does them. Don't ever put your approval on any thing that's not of God for you will be as guilty as those who commit the sin. God will not hold you guiltless when you stand before Him at the judgment.

Rom.5:9-10, We will be saved from the wrath of God through Jesus Christ. God will save those that follow Him and stay faithful and obedient to Him to the end. For when we were enemies and then became reconciled to God through Jesus Christ we will be saved by His life. He that is dead to sin is free from sin. Now you are to walk in newness of life. The old person is crucified with Him that the body of sin might be destroyed, that from now on we should not serve sin. If we are dead to sin then we will live with Him. Now you are dead to sin but alive unto God through Jesus Christ.

Verses 12-13, Let not sin reign in your body that you should obey it in the lust thereof. Don't yield your instruments of righteousness unto sin, but yield yourselves to God, totally. Don't let your mind, thoughts, mouth, feet, ears or any of your and life yield to sin and unrighteousness. We are going through tests and trials because the Bible tells us that. We can grow stronger through our problems and we can be over comers for the Lord. If we never had any problems then we wouldn't know that He could solve them and we wouldn't learn to trust Him. We also learn patience, hope, experience and how not to be ashamed. These are Christian graces that come from God our Father. Thank God for His love, mercy, grace and long suffering toward us, His children. Acts 25:22, We must through many tribulations enter into the Kingdom of God.

In Romans 18 God's wrath is upon all who know the truth but do not obey it, keep it or live it. You are a hypocrite if you confess with your mouth and do not believe in your heart and follow Him in all of His ways .God's wrath is upon those who deny Him, those who have never confessed Him as Lord and Savior and do all kind of evil and sin. It is not enough just to confess Him but we must believe and obey Him. You can't live by faith alone for faith without works is dead. You can't have one without the other for they go hand in hand. You have to become a new person when you come to Christ. All things are passed away and behold all things are become new. Then you become an heir to the Kingdom of God. God forgives all sins and cast them into the sea as far as the east is from the west never to remember them anymore.

Rom.8:1, Therefore there is now no condemnation to those who are in Christ Jesus who walk not after the flesh but after the Spirit. Now you have union with Him and you walk as He walked. They that walk after the flesh cannot please God. If anyone has not the Spirit of Christ he is none of His. For as many that are led by the Spirit of God are the children of God. We have this blessed assurance that nothing can separate us from the love of God which is in Jesus Christ our Lord. So don't let anyone or anything separate your love from Him. You can be separated from Him because of sin because sin will separate you from God but not His love for you. God said that He will not look upon sin and it will cause your prayers not to be heard or answered by God. God loves everyone but not their sin. He would not look upon His own Son Jesus, when He took upon His back the sin of the world. He turned His face momentarily. God hates sin.

Understand, there is a difference in the wrath of God and trials and tribulations. Even when we live for God and follow in Christ footsteps we will have trials and tribulations. We don't have to have the wrath of God come down upon us because of these troubles. II Thessalonians 1:4-5, We must endure all persecution and tribulations and have patience, faith and live holy to be counted worthy of the Kingdom of God for which we suffer also. This is how we escape the wrath of God. When we go through trials and troubles in this life we're not alone for God is with us and He will make a way for us for He said He would. He's our Keeper, our Salvation, our Strength, our Healer, Protector, our Guide, and our breathe of life, today tomorrow and forevermore. He loves us with an everlasting love.

There is danger in refusing correction from God. A person who remains stiffed necked after many rebukes will suddenly be destroyed without remedy. There will be no cure, no repair, no counteract for evil. Therefore disaster will over take him in an instant and he will suddenly be destroyed without remedy. Proverbs gives us warning against rejection, wisdom and corrections. The faithless will be fully paid for their ways. God said, My people would not listen to Me or submit to Me so I gave them over to a reprobate mind because of their stubborn hearts to follow their own devises. If God would do this for His chosen people, how much less do you think He will do to the people of today? God is not mocked for He will do what He said He would do and you can count on that for God is not a man that He should lie.

Most tragic refusal is rejecting Jesus Christ as your Savior and Lord. There's no turning back or chance after death. Hell will be the final destination for the lost and all who have rejected Christ. There will no way to correct that when you stand before Jesus Christ in the judgment. He will have to say to you, Sorry for I never knew you, depart from Me you workers of iniquity to the everlasting punishment in the lake of fire that burns with fire and brimstones. Then you will be reminded of all the times God warned you and Jesus called you to come follow Him and you refused. Please don't wait for today is the day of salvation. You may never have another chance for you may never live to see another day. Jesus Christ could come in the rapture to take His bride, the church out and you won't be ready or you could be taken suddenly by death and not be ready. There is a point of no return, after the rapture has taken place or after death. Accept Him now and live for Him here on this earth and then live forever with Him and all of the saints.

There is no excuse for doing wrong or sinning

God's wrath is against all mankind for sinning or denying Him, He will judge the world. The wrath of God is revealed from Heaven against all ungodliness and wickedness of man who supplies the truth by their wickedness. Since what may be made plain to them because God has made it plain to them. Men are without excuse not to know Him because you can see it in all of the creation. Romans 1:18-32 tells us all about it. Evidence of God surrounds everyone, His existence is everywhere in the world for what He has done. You can see the earth, sea, sky, stars, moon, sun, night and day, animals. Mankind, all kind of animals, the fowl of the air, all kind of insects, creatures in the sea and even a new born baby. He's not just a God of creation but a God of love, mercy long sufferings and grace. These people knew God was real. The Jews and the Gentiles alike but they wouldn't serve Him or give Him any glory. They became worthless and foolish. They exchanged the glory of the Immortal God for idol images made to look like man, birds, animals and reptiles.

God gave them over to their own sinful flesh and desires of their hearts. Sexual impurities, degrading of their bodies with another, they exchanged the truth for lies and worshipped and served created things more then the Creator. He gave them over to their shameful lusts. Women exchanged natural relations for unnatural ones. Men abandoned their natural affection to women for men. They received for themselves the penalty for their perversion. Men and women are still receiving their due penalty for sin of the flesh. There are many medical problem of the flesh such as aides, incurable diseases and even death because of the sin of the body. God made woman for man not man for man and woman for woman. He made woman to be a man's wife.

Since they didn't think it was worth while to worship God and to do what was right, God gave them over to a reprobate and corrupt mind to do whatever they wanted to do. God won't make you serve him or even make you do what's right for you have a free will choice, it's everyone's individual choice. No one will be held accountable for your choice but you. Even though they knew the penalty for their sins they still continued in their sins. To know to do good and not do it to you it is sin. Repent now and turn from your sins.

Beware lest you fall

Jude 6-7, And the angels who did not keep their position of authority and left their habitation fell. God has reserved them in chains now in darkness for judgment on that great day. If we fall away from God and the position He has called or placed us in then we will fall from grace and we will be lost like the angels are. If God spared not the angels who He made a little lower than Him then do you think He would spare human beings? In the same way Sodom and Gomorrah and the surrounding towns gave themselves up to sexual immorality and perversion and gave themselves for the punishment of eternal fire. They had rather go through the fire than to turn from their wicked ways and turn to the Lord. These people could have had it all but they choose to feed the lust of the flesh than to serve God. There's a judgment day coming for all, for everyone will stand before Jesus Christ and be judged.

Rev.12:8, Lucifer was the most beautiful angel of all and he was cast out of Heaven by God and his angels with him. Everyone has a leader and the angels followed the ole devil and were cast down with him. If you follow the wrong people they will lead you astray. Don't say that you would never fall for the wrong thing. Adam and Eve did and God walked and talked with them everyday. Eve sinned and persuaded Adam to follow her and they were both put out of the Garden of Eden. Be care when you think that you stand lest you fall.

Seven steps to Peter's fall for he was conceited, self confident, and boastful. He was a man of God and followed Christ for he loved his Lord. But he was weak and he denied Christ 3 times. Matt. 26:33, Peter said, though all men shall be offended of Thee, I will never be offended. When we got saved we made a vow to God to follow Jesus Christ and be faithful to Him all the days of our life. So many times problems or troubles come in our paths and we soon forget. That's what Peter did for he grew weak but he didn't stay in that condition for he repented.

When Jesus was in the garden He asked the disciples to watch and pray with Him for one hour. Jesus went to pray and then came out and found the disciples all asleep. He asked them, couldn't you have watched and prayed for one hour? He went back to pray again and came back to them again and found them asleep again. This showed their human weakness.

That's like Jesus asking us today. Can't you read and study My Words, pray and talk to Me? Can't you do it for one hour? What is your answer to Him? Are you so busy doing something else that you can't take the time to spend with the Lord?

Peter warmed himself, he was among the sinners and evil association instead of being with the believers. Do we ever find ourselves among these kinds of people? They can be a bad influence on Christians. That's why Jesus said to separate yourselves from these kinds of people. There are some Christians who fall and never come back to Christ. Beware lest you fall. Peter went on and denied Jesus 3 times. Peter had told Jesus that he would never deny Him. How quick we can forget the promises we make to God. Matt. 16:16 tells us about Peter confession to Christ. Thou are the Christ, the Son of the living God. Jesus told Peter, Thou are Peter and on this rock I will build My church and the gates of hell will nor prevail against it. Jesus Christ is Lord of forgiveness for He loves His children so.

Things we must do to keep us from falling away from serving Christ

Matt.26:41, Watch therefore and pray that you enter not into temptation. The spirit is willing but the flesh is weak. We are not to listen to our flesh but to the Holy Spirit of God. Let those that think they are strong take heed lest you fall. We are not strong within ourselves for God is our strength. He said to watch and pray. Be sober, vigilant because your adversary, the devil roams around like a roaring lion seeking whom he may devour. The devil will come at your weakest time to try to tempt you or to sway you wrong. We are to watch, stand strong be strong in faith, continue in prayer and watch in the same with thanksgiving. Always be thankful and praise God for what He has done. Keep yourselves in the love of God looking for the mercy of our Lord Jesus Christ unto eternal life. We have all sinned and fallen short of the glory of God. It's only because of His love, mercy, grace and His long suffering that any could make it into the Kingdom of God.

Rev.2:7, He who over comes will I give to eat of the tree of life in the midst of Paradise of God. Over comers I will give to eat the hidden manna, give them a white stone with a new name written on it. Over comers who keep My Word and works to the end will I give authority over the nations. We have to endure to the end to be over comers. Over comers will be clothed in white garments and I will not blot their names out of the Lamb's book of life but I will confess their names before My Father before His angels. You can see here that a Christian can fall from grace because Jesus said that He would not blot their names out of the Book of life. So if it was not possible to fall from grace then He would not have said that. I will write My name on them and I will sit with them on My throne. We will be perfect like Jesus, no more sin, sorrow, pain, trouble or death. We will have a perfect body and we will live forever in perfect peace and happiness. This is for all who endure to the end in Jesus. We will inherit all things, I will be their God and they shall be My sons and daughters.

There are many things we have to go through here on this earth but we must endure to the end and follow Jesus all of the way. You shall be hated by all people for My name sake, but they that endure to the end the same shall be saved. You must endure to the end and don't ever let anyone tell you anything different. You can't start this race and then stop. He will say to those who endure, Enter thou into the kingdom of Heaven prepared for you good and faithful servant. On the other hand He will have to say to the sinners and unsaved depart from Me you workers of iniquity into everlasting damnation.

Who can enter?

Rev.21:27, Nothing impure will enter in nor will anyone who does what is shameful or deceitful but only those whose names are written in the Lamb's book of life. Blessed are they that has washed their robes and have the right to the tree of life that they may enter into the gates to the city. Who shall ascend into the hills of the Lord? Who shall stand in His holy place? Those that have clean hands and a pure heart that has not lifted up their soul into vanity or sworn deceitfully. We have to love and serve him with our whole heart, mind, soul and strength. We cannot have any other god before Him. We have to keep our bodies holy and acceptable unto Him always. This is our reasonable service unto Him.

Who will not enter?

Outside are dogs, those who practice magic arts, fornicators, adulterers, sexual immoralities, murderers, idolaters and liars. Do not be deceived, nothing unclean or any sin will enter in. You can read all sinful things in, I Cor.6:9-10 and Gal.5:19-21.

I Cor.6; 11, If anyone has done any of these things in the past and have come to Jesus and repented and have turned from them and turned to Jesus then Christ will forgive you. Now you are washed in the blood of Jesus and you are sanctified, cleansed and justified as though you have never sinned and you can enter in. Therefore there is now no condemnation to those who are in Christ Jesus who walk not after the flesh but after the Spirit. You have been changed so make sure you endure to the end to enter into the Kingdom of Heaven. Now to Him that can keep you from falling, and to present you faultless, before the presence of His glory with joy, be glory forever.

Chapter 5

Good Can Come Out of Affliction

For it has been told us that if we follow Christ then we will suffer with Him. We have just seen that we can be over comers through Jesus Christ if we abide in Him. He will make a way for His children.

Rom.5:1-5, We can have peace and joy with God through sufferings. Therefore being justified by faith we have peace with God through our Lord Jesus Christ. By Whom we have access by faith into this grace where-in we stand and rejoice in hope, the glory of God. And not only so but we glory in tribulations also, knowing that tribulations works patience. Patience, works experience, experience works hope, and hope makes not ashamed because the love of God is shed abroad in our hearts by the Holy Spirit which is given unto us. We grow in our faith and strength and in the walk of God in this life. We learn through our tribulations how to trust God and lean on Him. If we had no problems how could we know that He could solve them? It is through our experience that we can really know Him. There is no where in the Word of God that He promised that we would have a bed of roses all of the time if we followed Jesus Christ but He did tell us that if we followed Him we would have trials and tribulations all of the days of our life here but He would make a way of escape for us and go with us through everyone. I know personally for He has done that over and over again for me. There are sorrows that we have to go through that we could not make it if He didn't make a way for us. We go through many things that we have no control over, like death of our loved ones and even many sicknesses and accidents of our loved ones or even ourselves.

There are benefits in sufferings

(1) Sufferings and trials teach Christians to be steadfast and determined. In situations we have a choice of giving up or doing all we can to make it through them. With God's help and strength we can make it through them. We could not do it on our own strength. He is our Refuge, our Healer, our very present help in time of trouble and our Salvation. (2) It teaches us hope and trust in God. For each trial and tribulation that we go through we learn that we can trust God because He has helped us before and we know we can trust Him to do it again. He is our source and strength in time of trouble. (3) It teaches us joy because we've seen God work through sufferings. We can have joy when we're going through troubles because the joy of the Lord is our strength. He didn't say that we'd have happiness but we can have joy. There is a different in joy and happiness. Happiness will go away for a season but joy is of the Lord and it is a lasting joy. In the book of James, he tells us to count it all joy when we fall into diver temptations knowing that the proving of our faith bring out the endurance, patience, and steadfastness and it will have full play and do a thorough work so that we can develop full development, lacking nothing. We will grow stronger in the Lord and learn to be an over comer. There are two ways we can handle problems, our way or God's way. Our way will fail but God's way will never fail. God's way teaches us many things. (4) It teaches us patience and experience. Rom.8:28, For we know all things work together for good to them that love God and are called according to His purpose. If you are God's child then He has called you and He has a purpose for you. We can't see many times how something can work together for good but God knows what He is doing. God has a plan for every life and every child of His.

I look back on my life and I can see now why I had to go through many things that I went through. At the time I just couldn't see how it could have been meant for good. The Word says we cannot go by feeling and what we see but we have to trust in Him. When we came to Him and He saved us then we are not ours anymore for we belong to Him now. Jesus paid a great price for us when He died. The trials that I went through before God used them to help the women at the prison where I worked. It was amazing to know how God had brought me out of my problems in life to be able to help someone else. Had I not have gone through those problems I would not have know how to help someone else. My problems were a preparation for the work at the prison. I could not have been as understanding nor could I have had patience to work with them. I looked at some of them and thought, if God had not have helped me through some of my problems I could have done some of the things they had done and could have been there in the prison with them. Don't ever think that you are so good that it can't happen to you. Many a good person is in prison but they got caught up in something and they became weak in themselves and committed a crime. God put a love in my heart for those women and I prayed with them many times. I took my Bible everyday and we had prayer before we began our work day till one day the officials called me in and said I couldn't do that anymore for we had to separate state and religion. Some of the devil's crowd was complaining. I did have to stop the group praying but they could not stop one on one praying. You see, the devil is working in every place and all of the time but God is there too and making a way of escape for His children. I knew that working there for the state there at the prison wasn't just a job to get paid but God had sent me there to help others. I thank God for that job. Many women went out of there a better person and the last I heard from some they were doing great. God has a plan for all of us and we need to follow that plan and trust Him with all of our heart, mind, soul and strength.

Ps.34:19, Many are the afflicted of the righteous but the Lord delivers them out of all of them.Ps.41:3 (NIV) The Lord will sustain them on their sickbed and restore them from their bed of sickness. God is our healer as well as our sustainer in all troubles. He does allow sickness to come upon us but He will deliver us again and make us well and whole. There are sicknesses that can lead to death but God is in control of that too. He does heal through death many times. He knows all about a person and He knows whether they will still serve Him if He heals them and they remain on earth. He is so full of mercy and grace. There have been many who have gone back out in sin after God has healed them and some never came back to Him. So I believe that He allows death to heal some because they are ready to go and if they lived and stayed they would have gone back in sin and would have been lost. I saw my sister do that several times. God healed her several times of cancer and she went back into sin. Then one day the cancer came back and she started down hill and she never was restored to health again here. She got her life back right with God and she finally told me not to pray for her healing again for she wanted to go home. I honored her decision and God took her home and she was totally healed through death. If God would have taken her years before she may not have been ready, and if He would have healed her and she would have lived longer she may would have fallen again because of the situation she was living in at her home. Only God knows but we know one thing, He never makes a mistake and He is full of mercy, love and grace. We should never question Him or complain about what He does.

Isa.43:2, When one passes through the waters I will be there and through the rivers I will be with you, they shall not flow over you. When you walk through the fire you shall not be burned neither shall the flames kindle upon you. This means to set you ablaze. When there seem to be no way at all and everything is looking down on you completely, He will be there to keep you safe in His care even in death. II Cor.12:9, Paul said, and He said unto me, My grace is sufficient for you for My strength is made perfect in weakness. God is our strength is weakness. We are still in the flesh even though we are led by the Spirit but He is strong and that's what we lean on, His strength.

Do you want the power of God living in you?

I Pet.4:12-13, Beloved think it not strange concerning the fiery trials which are to try you as though some strange thing happened to you. But rejoice in as much as you are partakers of Christ's suffering. There's glory just around the corner. When life gets difficult don't jump to conclusions that God isn't on the job. Instead, be glad that you're in the midst of what Christ experienced. This is a spiritual refining process with glory just around the corner. Be patient and wait on the Lord to do His work in you and others. No one likes to suffer. If it was up to us we would probably choose to enjoy nothing but ease and prosperity. The pain of life can be a great teacher. When we're in pain we're most likely to look beyond ourselves and look for wise solutions to our problems. Our neediness can drive us to God, both for comfort and to look for the lessons in afflictions. A sincere follower of God is willing to be taught wisdom and to look for the lessons in afflictions. When we're open to hidden gifts of God, of coming to the end of our rope we can actually be grateful for our trials knowing that we're coming through them with hope, peace, patience, experience, strength and more faith in God. James 5:1-2, Count them all joy when you fall into divers temptation or trials. Verse 12, Blessed is the one who endures temptations for they shall receive the gift of eternal life. We will receive the crown of life. James 5:11, We count them happy that endure trials and sufferings. God doesn't want his children to suffer but He loves us so much that He will allow whatever it takes to get our attention. Sometimes He uses strong Christians to reach the weaker Christians through their sufferings because of their faith in Him.

Christ wants us to have a relationship with Him because we love Him and not just for the benefits He gives. Often people are seeking the benefits of God such as peace, joy, love and going to Heaven. But they're not seeking the relationship with Him that's required to get the benefits from Him. Amos 5:4, God wants Christians to see Him not just the benefits. God wants a people who are looking for a relationship with Him, those who are willing to sacrifice for that relationship. God wants us to be willing to suffer for His sake. He has told us that, we must suffer many things in order to enter into the Kingdom of Heaven. God knows the benefits sufferings brings peace, joy and hope that shines brightly in a life of suffering. God uses suffering to produce deep and lasting peace, joy and hope.

Believers in the wilderness

Deut.8:3, And He humbled and suffered you to hunger and fed you with manna which you knew not neither did your fathers know that He might make you know that man could not live on bread alone but by every Word that proceeds out of the mouth of the Lord does he live. As believers in Christ, God takes us through the wilderness experiences. The time spent in the wilderness is never a happy one but we can have the joy of the Lord. It is here that the Lord humbles us, test and reveals to us the content or strength of our heart. It is all revealed to us in the wilderness experiences. Are we really dependant on God or self or someone else? Do we complain or question God why these things are happening to us? Do you feel that you don't deserve these trials? God's greatest plan and desire is to prepare us for the Promised Land that He has prepared for us. Our hearts has to be made right with Him completely to enter into the Kingdom of Heaven. Does this mean we have to be perfect? No, there's none perfect but Jesus Christ. But we have to strive to be perfect just as He is perfect. It can only be done God's way. Will you admit how needful these tests and trials are?

Will you allow this humbling testing and process to produce a saint of God that knows how to depend on Him completely? That's God's goal, what's your goal?

Deut.32:52, We see the Israelites all died in the wilderness because of sin. Abraham saw the Promised Land but could not go in. His disobedience kept him from entering into the land flowing with milk and honey and all of the beauty and good things. Moses had taught the Israelites and tried to equip them for the entrance there but they all failed because of sin and unbelief. God gave them everything they needed while in the wilderness. He supplied them with food, water and their shoes didn't even wear out. What is in your life to keep you out of the Promised Land, the Kingdom of Heaven?

John 1:23, John was a man, a fore runner of Jesus Christ crying in the wilderness. He said, I am the voice crying in the wilderness, make straight the way of the Lord as the prophet Isaiah has said before. John taught, repent, for the Kingdom of Heaven is at hand. Isa.40:3, Isaiah said, prepare the way of the Lord, make His path straight. John was preaching deep, heart felt and emotional. He felt what he preached and he lived it as well. It was more a command to the people for he knew the importance and necessity of living right and getting close to God. He went around crying in the wilderness so he felt the pain of the lost people. We can't just be religious but we have to have a relationship with Jesus Christ. A man and his message cannot be separated for they are one and the same. We have to live what we preach and teach. We have to feel the importance of telling the message of and ease and go into the wilderness where He can teach us what we need to know and what we need to do. This means forsaking your wants and find where the Lord needs you most. John had only one message and that was to repent. Repenting means to be sorry for your sins, turning from the direction you're going and turning to God for that's the right direction. Turn from sin to salvation, turn from self righteousness to God. Turn from religion to Christianity, die to self and follow God and live for Him. You can't have communication with Him without a relationship with Him. Repentance makes one to see himself as God sees them.

Isa.40:3, Mal.3:1, John 3:1-3, All of these tell the same story and truth, they all tell us to prepare the way. This means the road needs repairing in your life for Jesus is coming. Jesus paved the road for us so we know what we need to do. There is no excuse for failure. Jesus was in the wilderness for 40 days and nights and He never failed. You might be saying, but He was God. He was a man as well as God when He walked on earth. He was tested and tried above all that we can even imagine. No one has ever been through what He did for us. He suffered as man just as you and I are but He never sinned. When the devil tested Him Jesus told him that you can't live on bread alone but by every Word of God. Jesus was always listening to what His Father had to tell Him. Do you wait and listen to hear from God for what to say or where to go? When things go wrong, do you depend on Him for the answer? We need to wait on the Lord always for He has the answers. He can do anything but fail and His Word will come and always be on time. It is then you will experience true fulfillment and be an over comer for the Lord.

Why hang up your harps?

Ps.137:1-4, By the rivers of Babylon we sat and wept. That was the Israelites when we remembered Zion which is the city of Jerusalem city of David the sacred place. There on the popular trees we hung our harps. For there our captors asked for us songs, tormentors demanded songs of joy. They said, sing us one of the songs of them Lord in a foreign land. The Israelites were captive sad and cried, they had lost their joy but didn't totally forget God and that Zion was the city of God.

Sometimes things come our way, in fact lots of times out of our control. We cry, we complain and even lose our joy for a while. We feel we have lost our freedom and are in bondage. We too hang our harps on a willow tree so to speak. We see no good thing just the bad. But let's not forget Zion the place of God and how He blesses us over and over again. He's right there with you and He never leaves you. Be thankful in all things, not for all things but in all things because God is in control of our lives. No matter how bad things may get we still can have the joy of the Lord in our hearts. Remember, the joy of the Lord is your strength. When our hearts and minds are turned to Him then whatever we're going through will be made easier for us in the Lord. God is with us through the good and the bad. He's God on the mountain as well as God in the valley. He's the God of the day as well as the God of the night. If we didn't go through some bad times we wouldn't know that we could trust him. Talk comes easy when life's at it's best but it's down in the valley of the trials and temptations when our faith is put to the test. So don't give up or give into your problems, don't hang your harps on the willow tree. It doesn't hurt to cry but don't lose your joy or faith.

John 15; 11, These things have I spoken to you that your joy might remain in you and that your joy might be full. God doesn't take His joy from us when we have a problem. When His joy remains in us we can be full of joy, that's how God wants it to be. Paul said that he took pleasure in infirmities, in reproaches, in necessities, persecutions and in distresses for Christ sake, for when I am weak then I am strong, because His strength in me. The Lord said, My grace is sufficient for you for My strength is made perfect in weakness. We can sing songs in a foreign land. We can sing when it seem things are falling apart in our life all around us. We cannot lean on our strength but on His. When we start singing, praising the Lord and worshipping Him then we draw strength from the Lord and we forget out problems. We need to look at the problem solver and not on the problems. When we lean on His strength then we will have joy for the joy of the Lord is our strength.

This is my personal testimony about music in my life. If it had not been for music in my life I would have been most miserable. With any problem that come my way I could sit down at the piano and play the songs of Zion and sing about Jesus and lose myself totally in them. The problems didn't go away but God gave me peace, joy and comfort at that time of sorrows and troubles. He gave me the strength to go through them just as He said He would. He was my strength in my weakness. My mind was at rest in Him. He is still my strength, joy and happiness for He's the One I lean on and trust in. praise His Holy name. I don't have the problems that I had back then but I still go through many trials and I know I will continue to go through trials as long as I live in this flesh but He will see me through them all, for I have this confidence. We have to endure to the end to be saved and I am striving for that everyday that I live. There's coming a day when there won't be any problems, troubles, trials, tribulations, sickness or death. Keep trusting Jesus Christ and living for Him and doing His will and we will be in that land where there's happiness, joy, peace and we'll live with Jesus forever. Live everyday like it will be your last one here on this earth. God wants us to live in the fullness here. He wants us to prosper and be in good health just as our soul prospers. He longs to bless His children with good things. Is your soul prospering in the Lord?

Dark days

Jesus promised us there would be dark days to come our way at times. But He promised us another thing as well. He said He would lighten our darkness for He is our light. In Him there is no darkness. He has told us that we are the light of the world so we need to be light for those who are going through dark places in their lives. God works through His people. We know Job faced many dark places in his life. God allowed the devil to try him because He knew Job's heart and that he would stay true to Him. Does God know that about you? He knows our hearts and our desires and He judges us from the heart. Job said in 30:26, I looked for good and there was evil all around me and when I waited for the light and darkness came. Job was an upright man, a man of God. He loved the Lord and did nothing wrong in His sight. He knew that God had allowed these things to come upon him to test him but he also knew that God would always be there for him and make a way for him to see the light.

Ps.88:6, David faced dark places as well as Job. He said to God, and said in verse 13, I am counted with them that go down to the pit. I am a man that has no strength. David went through a lot of dark places. Some of them he caused himself and brought on himself like we do many times in this life. Some of the dark places were brought on by sin and some were for testing. But he knew that God was with him and would answer his prayers when he called on Him. Even though he went to the lowest pit he hung on to God. He said, in all the days of trouble I will call on the Lord for He will answer me. For God has heard me and attended to the voice of my supplications. My soul waits only upon God and my expectations are from Him. We are to expect to hear from God when we call upon him. It's according to our faith when we call upon Him whether He will give us what we ask. The Bible teaches us never to doubt when we ask Him for anything. If we expect to get from the dark side to the light we have to trust Him. We have to do it His way and not ours.

John 8:12, Jesus said, I am the light of the world. They that follow Me shall not walk in darkness but shall have the light of life. We may have darkness for a while but we know that joy comes in the morning. There is light in darkness when we have Jesus for He is the light. In the world you shall have tribulations but be of good cheer for I have overcome the world. In Me you shall have peace. No matter what we're going through He will do what He promises. Only God can give this kind of peace, you won't find it in the world or in anyone else. John 16:20, He said that our sorrows will be turned into joy. Acts 14:22, Paul told the disciples to continue on in the faith for we must suffer many tribulations in order to enter into the Kingdom of God. James1:12, Blessed is the man that endures temptation for when he is tried he shall receive the crown of life which the Lord has promised them that love Him.

Remember, that good can come out of afflictions. You will be stronger in the Lord. Your faith will be stronger and you will know that you can lean and trust in the Lord. All things work together for good to those that love the Lord and are called according to His purpose. Say in all truth, I will live for you Lord, no matter what comes my way for I know you are in control. I will serve you because I love You. I don't serve You because I have to but I serve you because I want to.

Chapter 6

Do you need To Change Your Oil?

*O*il evaporates if it's not replenished regularly. It will eventually disappear, sometimes there's a leak and it leaks out and sometimes the wrong oil is used. Do you have holes in your vessel? Is your oil black with sin? If you don't have a good relationship with Jesus Christ, read and study His Word and live a Spiritual life with Him on a daily basic then you will not or do not have the proper oil. You need to change your oil. Your Christian walk with Him will not work without having Jesus in your heart and life all of the time.

Sometimes we have holes of bitterness in our lives. There may be unforgiveness in your heart. If you don't forgive others then Christ won't forgive you either. Some walk around with self-pity, feeling sorry for themselves, feeling down and depressed, all washed up and all faith is gone. Corrupt language or evil speaking and any other sin can blacken your oil. When your oil gets black you have to change it. You can't make it into the Kingdom of Heaven with black oil. Your oil has to be clean and pure to make in into the Kingdom. Be careful not to let these things creep into your lives and let the oil of the Holy Spirit leak out. The Holy Spirit will not live in a temple of sin. It's the little foxes that spoil the vine so be careful of them. Epe.4:27, Give no place to the devil. If you let him ride then he will want to drive.

Chapters 4 of Ephesians tell us we are prisoners of the Lord so walk worthy of the work that He has called you to do. This chapter tells us how to live, what to do and what to say. It is full of pure oil. Verse 30, grieve not the Spirit of God. We know that any sin grieves Him. Don't let sin take

55

you unaware but be on your guard and flee from the devil. Draw near to God and He will draw near to you. Don't listen to your flesh but listen to the Holy Spirit for He will lead and guide you into all truth. If you don't feel and know what's wrong listen to the Holy Spirit. Take care of your oil, keep it clean and pure. The oil we are talking about here is your soul so keep it with all of your might.

II Tim.3:5, Paul said, some people have a form of godliness but deny the power thereof. Lets not be one of those people. He said to turn away from such people. There's power in the Holy Spirit and it has been given to God's children to use for His Kingdom and to keep us in line with Him. Luke 12; 48, To whom much is given much is required. Before God will give you more He looks to see what you've done with what He has given you. We are God's hands, feet and mouth and He wants to use us for His kingdom here on earth. Can He trust you with the gifts He has for you? God will not give you double portions if you're hanging on to yesterday's weights. Let go and let God move in your life and let Him use you for His glory. Phil.3; 13, Forgetting those things which are behind you and reach for those things which are ahead. Don't look at your failures and mistakes or weaknesses or even wasted time because you can't change what's in your pass but press on, striving for the things that God has for you and press toward the goal to win. Maybe un-forgiveness, anger, bitterness, strife, hatred or any other sin is keeping you from being filled with the Holy Spirit. You have to get rid of all of the bad stuff and sin in your life. Your oil will grow thin under the heat and Spiritual warfare. That's why we must stay in God's Word and pray always. It's the only way to keep your oil clean and pure. Make sure you have a good relationship with Jesus Christ. Stay in communication with Him. Keep your oil tank full at all times to be able to survive this life and have joy.

Let's Go on a Journey

II Kings 2, We're going from salvation, growing in the Lord, surrendering all to Him, dying to self completely and then Spiritual visions and place of miracles. First, we're going to look at <u>Gilgal,</u> a place of religious activity with no super natural power. Gilgal was a place of comfort and a place where you could just lay back. It was a place where you could forget your old life. The first Church of Gilgal. Christians are just satisfied with just being born again and the religious activity that's going on, the fun part.

Never growing or maturing in the Lord or seeking the Holy Spirit. This was one of the places that Elijah traveled to, where the cloud by day and the fire by night were no longer evident. Elisha was traveling with him and Elijah told him to stay there while he traveled on but Elisha told him no. He was going with him for he wanted a double portion of what he had. He wanted that anointing that Elijah had, he wanted to be like him. Elijah was a shadow of Jesus Christ and Elisha was a type of what you and I should be. As Christians we should always want to follow Jesus wherever He goes.

The Lord sent Elijah to <u>Bethel</u>. This was a place where you could surrender and yield all to God, A place of dying to self, a place of surrender to God. Here you could find forgiveness and learn the ways to live a life of happiness. You learn the basic of a Christian life. You're taught you're growing and have a more desire to follow Christ, but you're not living in the fullness of God as He desires for you. You've not been taught or experienced the fullness of God at this point. This is the house of God and you can stop here or go ahead for more and the anointing and blessings of God. This is where Abraham pitched his tent to make decisions to live for God. Samuel first heard the voice of God here. It's a place where Saul rejected the Word of God and lost everything including his kingdom. Don't go so far and then quit for you must endure to the end to be saved so we must go on and learn more and let our faith grow deeper in the Lord. We have the same choice as Elisha did, we can go on further and receive more of the Lord and receive the Holy Spirit and His anointing or we can just stay here at Bethel.

We will go on to <u>Jericho</u>, a place of actions and warfare. It was in this vicinity that Jesus faced the devil for 40 days and nights being tempted of him in the wilderness. Many trials will follow us if we follow Jesus Christ. A man was beaten and robbed and left for dead on the road to Jericho. We know two people passed him by and wouldn't help him. One was a priest, one was a Levite but the one that stopped and helped him was a good Samaritan. He took care of his wounds and took him to a place where he could get the right care and even left some money for him. Does this sound like a familiar story? There are some Christians as well as non-Christians in need today and who will help? Do you pass the needy by and not help? Jesus said, whatever you do for others you are doing as unto Me. We know in Joshua 6, the walls of Jericho came down. When the people did what God told them to do, march around the walls seven times, then the walls fell down. They couldn't do just half of what He said but they had to obey completely. Obeying Him partially is not good enough. Jesus went all the way for us and we have to do the same for Him. God wants all of you, not just part of you. Trust Him fully, looking to Him for everything. You need to give up the old so God can perform the new in your life.

Warfare surrounds the birth of a miracle. The devil will oppose and attack you in anyway he can if you let him. Being born again is a miracle, the greatest miracle ever happened. You know it's the darkest before the dawn. Weeping may last for the night but joy comes in the morning. He will attack your finances, your body, mind, family, your ministry and your faith if you will let him. Some times the forces of hell will attack you. James 4:7, Submit to God, resist the devil and he will flee from you, draw near to God and He will draw near to you. Don't delay your journey because your victory is on the way. Don't be sold out, believe and act on it. Don't be distracted by tour flesh for distraction is the enemy of your soul. The devil likes to cause you all of the problems that he can. Many fall away just before they finish the journey. Many fall away just before God brings their blessings. Keep your mind and heart on the Lord. God will give you the power to move on to victory. He will never leave or forsake you and you can depend on this.

Our next stop is <u>Jordan.</u> Jordan is a place of Spiritual visions, a place of growth, a place of faith, a place of total death to self, a place of miracles and a place of obedience. When you can see with the eyes of faith the promises begins to come your way with power. Prayer is the key to Heaven but faith unlocks the door. Jesus began His ministry in Jordan. He was filled with the Holy Spirit. John the Baptist saw the Holy Spirit in Jordan, he saw a dove from the shoulder of Jesus. He baptized Jesus in the Jordan River. Elisha was still with Elijah and he received his double portion in Jordan. Jordan was a well watered land that Lot chose.

Leon, my dear loving husband, received his healing in 2002 at Spiritual Jordan. I'm so glad we didn't atop at Gilgal, Bethel or Jericho but went on to Jordan. Jordan is a Spiritual place where we learned to totally depend on God, it's a place of miracles, power, and growth in the Lord Jesus Christ. It's a place of Spiritual visions, a place where we see through the eyes of faith and not by sight or feelings. I thank God and I praise Him for all of the things He has taught us through our traveling with Him through the years.

I'm so excited that we didn't stop when we first were born again for God has tremendously blessed us for going on in Him. I thank God that we kept our minds and hearts on Him through all of devastating sickness of my husband. I thank God that we didn't give up or give in to the negative feeling of so many other people. I thank God that we didn't accept the doctors report but we stood on the Word of God. I shall live and not die and declare the works of the Lord. God is in control for He is the God that heals Me. By His stripes we are healed. Trust in the Lord with all of your heart and lean not upon your own understanding in all your ways acknowledge Him and He will direct your ways. There were so many more scriptures that we stood on during his sickness and we did not sway from them. God gave us peace and strength to go through it together. Jesus said, if two ask anything in My name I will do it. The two of us continued to agree together and God worked a miracle. All praise and glory goes to Him for everything. With our eyes of faith we began to see the promises of God reveal it right before us. What we prayed and believed for came to pass by the love, mercies and grace of God. We began to see the promises of Heaven that were ours. When the Words said, I will live and not die and declare the works of the Lord, we stood on it and would not let it go. When it looked the darkest, perfect peace came and held us and carried us through. That was our Spiritual Jordan, Jesus brought us through. Praise the Lord.

Will you be an Elisha and follow Jesus and abide in Him? He saw Elijah ascend up to Heaven and he received his double portion... He endured to the end and that's what we have to do to receive the rewards that Jesus has for us, His children. We can be a force for God that will shake the Heavens and the earth. Will you follow Jesus Christ always?

Ps. 89:21, God said, I have found David, My servant with My Holy oil I have anointed him. Verse 34, my covenant I will not break nor alter the thing that is gone out of my mouth. God's promises are for His children but the anointing carries a price. It will cost you total death to self. We have to die daily to self and live totally for Him. We have to be lead by the Holy Spirit in everything we say and do and even where we go. I Cor.15:31, The price is total death to self, die daily to self. Luke 9:23, All worldly desires have to go. Do not allow anything in your life to be disrespectful to God, or be disobedient to Him. Eze.36; 27, And I will put My Spirit in you and cause you to walk in My statues and you shall keep My commandments. Acts 1:8, But you shall receive power after that the Holy Spirit is come upon you and you shall be witnesses unto Me both in Jerusalem and in all Judea and in Samaria and unto the uttermost part of the earth. We have God's Spiritual equipment, so we need to use it.

God didn't give us a price to big to pay. He gave us oil that will never have to be changed or will never run out if we abide in Him forever. Just as Elisha followed Elijah we are to follow Christ all of the way. I Cor.3; 16, Know you not that you are the temple of God and the Spirit of God dwells in you. If you should lose the anointing of God then you will have to repent and be refilled with new oil again. If you have never been filled then you need to be filled with this new, clean and pure oil of the Holy Spirit. If your oil is burnt, dirty or has leaked out, it will cause your motor to run rough and lose strength, and then you need a refilling of oil. Isa.40:31, They that wait upon the Lord shall renew their strength. Without the Holy Spirit living in us we are none of His. How is your oil? Do you need a change? Keep your vessel full with clean, pure oil. Make what's wrong in your life, right.

I would like to give you this warning about the Holy Spirit. Gen.6; 3, God said, My Spirit shall not always strive with man. A person can only come to the Lord when the Spirit of God draws them to Him. You can't get saved anytime you want to. You have to call on God and ask. I Sam.16:14, The Spirit of God departed from Saul and he was the anointed king by God. But he sinned and God took His Spirit from him. You can lose the anointing just as Saul because of sin in your life. Be sure your sins find you out.

There are three Anointing

1- Leper's anointing, comes by accepting Jesus Christ as your Savior

2- Priestly Anointing, comes by fellowship with Jesus

3- Kingly Anointing, comes by obedience

Leper's anointing is salvation. The only cure for sin is the blood of Jesus Christ. The Holy Spirit convicts a person of sin and draws them to Christ. You can be saved always if you continue in the Lord Jesus Christ or you can lose it if you choose not to follow Him. Sin will separate you from God. He will not leave you but you can pull away from Him. You can lose the oil of salvation. In Revelation Jesus said I will blot your name out of the Lamb's book of life because of sin.

Priestly anointing is the presence or fellowship. This is to be renewed daily. It will bring you into the presence of God. It's one with a ministry and everyone should have a ministry in the work of the Lord. If you are leading souls to Christ then you have a ministry. We are all priests unto God, priestly anointing is being baptized in the Holy Ghost.

Kingly anointing is when God gives you a Word for that moment and you receive and speak it. You have the anointing of healing, casting out demons and works of miracles. This is the most powerful of the three anointing. With this one comes complete obedience to Jesus Christ in all things and complete death to self. God's Word is forever settled in Heaven and it's forever true. It's from God so believe and receive it.

How far do you want to go with God?

Acts 1:8, You shall receive power after the Holy Ghost shall come upon you and you shall be My witness everywhere. Check you oil. Only when you abandon self totally, empting yourself completely of anything that's not of God, can you be filled with God's presence, total death to self. Began every morning by inviting the Holy Spirit to come in and walk with you through out the day. Be like David said, early will I seek you Lord, my soul thirst for you, my flesh longs for You. Start now and experience the presence of the Holy Spirit. Allow Him to change your hearing, speech, vision, walk, and every action and every part of your being. Acts teaches us that nothing can take the place of a personal relationship with the Holy Spirit. The Spirit of Elijah was resting on Elisha. Is Jesus Spirit resting on you? HE IS REAL. Where are you in your walk with the Lord, Gilal, Bethel, Jericho or Jordan? Don't cut yourself short and stop your journey before you reach the end. Jesus went all the way for you so you need to go all of the way with Him. I can assure you that you will never regret it.

Make sure you're going the right way

There is a way that seems right in the eyes of man but in the end it leads to death. God said, My people are destroyed for lack of knowledge because they have rejected it. Don't just listen to the Word and deceive yourselves but do what it says. Anyone who hears the Word and doesn't do what it says is like a person who looks in a mirror and after he looks at himself he goes and immediately forgets what he looks like or saw. If anyone considers himself religious and does not keep his tongue he deceives himself and his religion is in vain or worthless. The tongue is a fire, a world of evil and it corrupts the whole person. The tongue has the power of life and death and those who love it will eat of it. What you say is what you get. What's inside will come out of your mouth. If we will listen to our words we're sure to find out what our inner source really is and that will lead us to try to tame our unruly tongue. Matt.11:7, What goes into a man's mouth does not make him unclean but what comes out of his mouth makes him unclean.

Luke 14:33-34, if any of you does not give up everything he cannot be My disciple. Salt is good but if it loses it flavor, how can it be salty again? It is fit for neither for the soil nor for the manure pile, for it is thrown out. Your attitude should be the same as salt, like Jesus Christ, a sweet Savor. Paul's prayer was that our love would grow more and more in the knowledge and insight. So that you may be able to discern what is best and may be pure, blameless until the day of Christ, being filled with the fruit of righteousness that comes from and through Jesus Christ to the glory and praise of God. We should do nothing out of selfish ambition or vain conceit but in humility, considering others better than ourselves. Each of you should look not only to your own interest but also to the interest of others. We are to continue to work out our own salvation with fear and trembling. James 4; 4, Anyone who has friendship with the world is an enemy of God. Never say what you will or will not do for James says that we should say, if it's God's will we will do this or that. Anyone who knows to do good and doesn't do it to them it is sin. We can't live as the world lives and please God. We are either for God or against Him. Jesus said that if we were lukewarm that He would spew us out of His mouth, meaning that we make Him sick. We have to be either cold or hot. I John 1:6 If we claim to have fellowship with God and walk in darkness we lie and the truth is not in us. If you say you know Him and don't keep His commandments, you are a liar and the truth is not in you. Whosoever claims to live in Him must also walk as Jesus did. Do not love the world or anything in it. I John 1: 4-5, If anyone love the world the love of the Father is not in him. The world and its desires pass away but the one who does the will of God will live forever. I John 3:6-10, No one who lives in Him keeps on sinning, no one who continues to sin has Him, either seen Him or known Him. He who does right is righteous just as He is righteous. He who does what is sinful is of the devil. No one who is born of God will continue to sin because God's seed remains in him. This is how we can know who are the children of God and who are the children of the devil. Anyone who does not what is right is not a child of God nor is anyone who does not love his brother (or sister) I believe this means spiritual and blood kin for we are to love everyone.

Jesus said, That if we can't love our brother how can we love Him? Anyone who does not love does not know God because He is love. Prov.16:17, The highway of the upright avoids or shuns evil. He who guards his way guards his life. There is a way that seems right to a man but in the end it leads to death. What we may think is right sometimes may not be. If Jesus wouldn't do it then it would be wrong for us too. .It has to line up with the Word of God, the Bible. The Word is our guide line and road map and we have to follow it. There are no short cuts in serving God and getting to Heaven to live with Him. We have to do it God's way. It's the best and only way. We will never be disappointed if we go the right way. In the end will be complete joy, peace and happiness. It will all be perfect health, wealth, love and life everlasting with Jesus and all of the saints of God.

Lip service and nor sincerity of heart

What does it profit my brethren though a man say he has faith and have not works? Can faith save him? Faith without works is dead being alone. It works together, neither one can stand alone for they go together hand in hand. Fervent or burning lips and a wicked heart are like an earthen vessel over laid with silver dross, it fades away. Ezek.33:31, they shall come in and hear and sit down before Me as My people but they will not obey My Words. For with their mouth they show much love but their heart goes after their covetousness. They just come to get something they want but they are not sincere. For they hear the Words but they don't do them. Matt.7:21, Not all who call Me l Lord, Lord shall enter into the Kingdom of Heaven, but just those who do the will of My Father which is in Heaven. It is written that people honor Me with their lips but their hearts are far from Me. They profess that they know Me but in works they deny Me being abominable or hateful and disobedient, unto all good works. Morally abandoned, wicked and rejected. Let us not love in word neither in tongue but in deed and in truth. Why do you call me Lord, Lord and do not the things which I say.

Our hope is built on Jesus Christ. All who repent and forsake their ways and sins will find forgiveness and restoration through Jesus Christ. God is watching you. You may fool a lot of people and even yourself but God knows your heart and your desires and you can't fool Him. Do not trust in your wickedness but trust in God. False trust, worldly wisdom and self confidence have taken over a lot of Christians. You believe in God but you don't live for Him or give Him first place in your heart and life. You do not trust Him completely. You say you have faith in God but you have no works and that's not good enough. You have to have faith with works. Prov.28:26, Whoever trust in their own way is a fool. There is nothing covered that shall not be revealed. God even knows our thoughts. You cannot serve God and the devil. You will fall because you can't serve two masters. Jesus said that He would not live in a temple, a body that was filled with sin. Remember, the devil believes in God and trembles. Lip service is not good enough. We must serve God from the sincerity of our hearts with love and obedience. If you believe in Him why wouldn't you want to serve Him with your whole life? How is it that you can't love Him enough to serve Him? Whatever you need to change do it before it's too late. Give it all to Jesus for He loves you so make what's wrong in your life right with Him.

Chapter 7

From The Beginning it was Not So

From the beginning there was no sin. God made everything perfect and made man in the image of Himself. Adam and Eve were made perfect. They knew no sin because there was no sin around them any place. It was God's will that men and women would live in a perfect and beautiful place. They were to enjoy life and multiply it with children and all living things. Sin came when Eve was tempted of the ole serpent and then she persuaded her husband Adam to sin along with her. That's the way sin is today, bad influences rubs off on others. Adam and Eve should have followed God because He was nothing but good but instead they were tempted of the devil and yielded to him. Ask yourself this question, who are you following God or the devil?

Matt.19:4-18, God made male and female in the beginning. God made the first marriage with Adam and Eve. They were made perfect. God made the first marriage and the first home. Because of this a man would leave his mother and father and mother and would cleave to his wife and they would become one flesh. They are no more twain but one flesh. What God has joined together let no man put asunder or do away with. God did not plan for man and wife to ever be separated in the beginning. The question was asked of the Pharisees to Jesus, why did Moses then command to give a writing of divorcement and to put her away, or leave her? Jesus said, Because of the hardness of your hearts he suffered you to put away, or leave your wife. But, from the beginning it was not so. Jesus said, But I say unto you, whosoever shall put away his wife except for fornication and shall marry another commits adultery and whosoever marries her that is put away commits adultery also. His disciples asked Him, then in a case

65

like this it's good not to marry? Jesus said to them, All men cannot receive this saying except to whom it is given. Verse 12, Let them that are able to accept this, accept this. I Cor.7:9, If a person cannot contain themselves it is better to marry than to burn. This means to burn with passion and then commit sin. We know God has said that He hates divorce but He hates all sin. He said He hates pride, the lust of the flesh, lust of the eyes, pride of life, and He hates lies. These things are not of the Father but are of the world and the father of the world which is the devil.

We know in the beginning there was no sin for God made everything perfect and beautiful and that's how He wanted it to stay. When Adam and Eve sinned it brought the curse of sin and judgment upon the earth. Sin has gotten worse and worse as time has gone by. In verse 18 more sins have been committed and are listed here, murder, stealing, lying, disobedient to parents as well as adultery. Jesus said, we should not kill, steal, bear false witness, and commit adultery or any other sin. This is what He said for us to do, we should love our neighbor as ourselves and honor our parents. Sin is sin for there is no sin bigger than the other in God's sight. God hates all sin. He did not make sin nor did He cause sin in any way. God is good and everything He does is good.

God hates spiritual pride

Luke 18:1, The Pharisees stood and prayed, O God, I am thankful that I am not like other people, robbers, crooks, adulterers or like the this tax man the Republican. Verses 13-14, The Republican prayed in humility, for he felt so unworthy, God be merciful to me a sinner. Jesus said, this man went home right with God. He was justified as though he had never sinned. Everyone who exalts themselves shall be made humble and those who humble themselves shall be exalted. It is better for you to humble yourself than for Jesus to humble you. There are consequences for every sin that you commit. God does have a way of humbling you. Don't ever think more highly of yourself than you are for this is pride and God hates pride. Don't be so spiritual minded that that you think that you can't make a mistake and fall. Beware lest you fall. Prov.29:23, A man's pride can bring him low but honor shall uphold in Spirit. Ps.7:11, God is angry with the wicked everyday. Rom.1:18, For the wrath of God is revealed from Heaven against all unrighteousness and ungodliness of men, who holds the truth in unrighteousness. These people know the truth but don't abide by it. Don't be deceived with vain words for because of these things, any sin, comes the wrath of God upon the children of disobedience. Mal.4:1, Behold the day comes that shall burn like an oven and all of the proud, yes, all that do wicked shall be stubble and the day that comes shall burn them up says the Lord of hosts. It shall leave them neither root nor branch. He's talking about hell here. God has made another beautiful place called Heaven and it's for the redeemed and faithful followers but He has also made a place for the wicked and the unbelieving and that's hell. Heb,10:31, It is a fearful thing to fall into the hands of the living God.

Now back to the marriage and divorce. If men and women would wait on God and let Him choose the right spouses, there would be far less divorces. He said not to be unequally yoked together for what has a Christian or the believer have in common with the unbeliever? God said what He has joined together let no one put asunder or separate. Not all marriages are put together by God. Most marriages today aren't. Marriage is a very sacred thing in God's sight and it should be in everyone's eyes. We should keep marriages sacred and holy with love, compassion, understanding, honor and respect for each other in all things. Death of a spouse is easier to go through than divorce because you have no control over death. Divorce causes a lot of hurt, guilt feelings and feelings of not belonging. The Church family judges you harshly and even condemns. It's like you can be forgiven for all other sins but not divorce. We all know that God said that He hates divorce but He also hates all sins. You have to remember that we're not living under the law anymore but we are living under grace. Some Christians are still trying to live under the law. When Jesus came He fulfilled the law for He became the sacrifice for our sins. Now we still have the commandments and He didn't condemn them for they are a school master for us to learn from. There are many who have forsaken the gospel and Jesus Christ because they were condemned because of divorce. They can go to church and give of their money but can't sing in the choir or have a position anyplace in the church. You don't know the situation people are in so who are you to condemn? Many stay in an abused marriage or in a marriage where their spouse is unfaithful because they are taught that they can't get out of it and many lose their lives because of staying in that kind of situation. I can't believe that God wants His children living in this kind of situation.

I know my first marriage of 15 years was hell on earth but it was taught to me that I was to stay in it or I'd be hell bound. Well, I stay until death parted us. He was unfaithful to me for all of those years, an alcoholic, hit me many times and I am still wearing the scars. I thought surely I was going to die first, but God spared me. The only good that came out of that marriage are four wonderful girls. I married young and out of the will of God so He didn't put this marriage together. So if I would have left I wouldn't have been putting asunder what God had joined together. It was our choosing and the pastor just spoke what was written in his little book. I believe you have to take the whole Word of God and not just part of it. Now, I'm surely not recommending you to get a divorce for it's between you and God. I'm just saying, read and study the whole Word of God and not just take the words of men and women. You can see for yourself and God will lead you. There's a scripture that says this, blessed are they that don't condemn themselves for the things that they approve of, that's in the book of Cor. If you have condemned someone for divorce then I would ask you, to ask forgiveness, for you just don't know the details or situations. If you have never been in a situation then you don't know what you would do until you face the same problem. We will all reap what we sow and there's always a penalty for sin.

There will never be another perfect marriage here on this earth since Adam and Eve because of sin. But we can strive to make a good one. We have the power in Jesus Christ to overcome the evil in this world. It's so wonderful to be married to such a great Christian man, one who loves God first and me second. I give God all of the glory. I know that God did put our marriage together and He has blessed us over and over again. Staying in the Word of God and praying together is the weapons that hold us so tightly together and we try so hard to stay in one accord. Do we have problems? Yes, but we overcome them and come into agreement with our disagreements.

Marriage outside of God's will

When a man and woman come together outside of God's will it is wrong from the very beginning and most of the marriages will not last or work. Marriage is a team work. You are really asking for trouble. I can say this because I've been there. If one is a believer and the other is not then you're unequally yoked. There is no fellowship in a believer and an unbeliever.

There is a penalty for making the wrong choices in marriage and anything else. God will forgive but you still have a price to pay. God has a plan for all of His children so why mess it up? I know I messed His plan up for me because I know for sure that God called me when I was eleven years old to do a work. I didn't know what but I remember when He called me. I didn't heed the call and on top of that I really messed up and did my own thing. I praise God that He kept His hands upon me all of these years and still gave me a work to do for Him. God does not repent of His calling the Word tells us. I could have been a Missionary, I just don't know but God knew my heart then and He knows it now. I have always wanted to serve Him. After all of those wasted years God still gave me my heart's desire. I always wanted a Christian husband, one who would put Him first and then I knew that he would put me second place in his life. We've been married now for 25 years. I can say with all honesty that it has been a great 25 years. We started in the singing ministry even before we were married and have been in God's ministry every since.

If you would just listen to God in the beginning about marriage and all phases of your life then you can live in His perfect will. I can never live in His perfect will because I messed up in the beginning and messed up His plans He had for me. I now live in His permissible will. He forgave me of all of my mistakes and gave me another chance so He had another plan for me. I will praise Him forever that He didn't throw me away. He didn't throw the clay away but He molded it again, cleaned it up and made it like new. I can't turn back the clock or change anything in my past but I can go on from this day forth doing the things He has called me to do now. He said, whosoever looks back at the plow is not worthy of the Kingdom of Heaven. When He forgives He forgets, never to remember our sins or wrongs anymore. God is my source and my husband is my second source of life. We have pleasure together and it's all because of Jesus Christ our Lord and Savior. We don't have to look for pleasure for we have it within ourselves with God.

When you marry out of God's will not only will you get hurt but your children, your family and your friends as well. I believe the children get the biggest hurt. Choose God first in your life and then lean and trust Him for all of the other decisions you have to make. God does all things well and He never makes a mistake. A bad marriage causes a lot of sufferings, afflictions, grief, regrets, tears of sorrow, hate, debt, financial problems and so, on and on.

Lets compare a bad marriage to the city of Jerusalem

Lam.3:39-49, Why should any living man complain when he is punished for sin? The Israelites were very disobedient group of people, they just wouldn't listen to what God was saying through Jeremiah the prophet. They wanted to do their thing and go their way. Then they couldn't understand when God would punish them for their sins. Jeremiah said, let us examine ourselves, our ways and test them and let us return to the Lord. Let us lift up our hearts and our hands to God in Heaven and say, we have sinned and rebelled and you have not forgiven. Lord you have covered yourself with a cloud so that no prayer can get through. My eyes will flow with tears unceasingly, without relief until the Lord looks down from Heaven and sees. Because of unbelief, sin and disobedience here in Lamentations the Israelites went through much sorrow and grief. Lamentation means to cry out in grief, tears of sorrow, pain, sufferings, regrets, to weep and mourn. This is how a bad marriage is. You're in it and it seems there is no way out and you live in it from day to day and it never gets any better. You pray and it seems God is not listening and is no where near you. What's so bad is the fact that you can't blame anyone but yourself for being in this condition. You can't blame God for you didn't seek Him in the first place. Now you have to come to a place in your life where you will have to choose again, whether to stay in the mess or get out. Now you really have to seek God for the answer and which way to go. You'll be like the Israelites, you will cry tears of sorrow and grief until the Lord looks down from Heaven to help you. He will help you because He loves and cares for you. He knows your heart whether it's pure and if your desire is to serve and follow Him or whether you just want out of the mess you put yourself in. God waits until we are sincere with Him to hear and answer our prayers.

Lam. 3:19-20, Jeremiah remembered how he did his own will and not God's will. He took on the misery of Jerusalem as though it was his own doings. He had compassion on them because he knew he had made the mistake of being disobedient to God also. He said that he remembered his afflictions and his wandering, the bitterness and the shame of his self-will. We need to have compassion on those who are in such situations just as though it was happening to us. Don't be so high minded and think you're so spiritual that you're no good to anyone else. Remember what Jesus said, those that exalt themselves He shall humble them. He knows just what to do to humble you.

Through it all there is hope for you in the Lord

Lam.3:21-26 and 55-61, The prophet Jeremiah turns to hope with one word. <u>YET</u>, this I recall to mind and therefore I have hope, because of the Lord's great love we are not consumed for His compassions never fail. They are new every morning, great is Your faithfulness. I say to myself, the Lord is my portion, therefore I will wait on Him. The Lord is good to them that have hope in Him. It is good to wait on the Lord patiently and quietly for the salvation of the Lord. Even though you have made a mistake and you feel the water is over your head, do as Jeremiah did. He said, I called on Your name Lord from the depth of the pit. You heard my plea, do not close your ears to the cry of relief. You came when I called you and said, do not fear. Oh Lord, You took my case, You redeemed my life. You have seen O Lord the wrong done to me, uphold my case. You have seen the depth of their vengeance, all their plots against me. O Lord, You have heard their insults and all their plots against me. Praise God for His mercy, grace and His love toward us. You know, outside of the will of God's there is so little joy, little honor, little happiness, little good living and lots of hell on earth. There is little to no peace without God in your heart and life. There is happiness in sin for a season but it quickly goes away.

Yet, as Jeremiah said, yet, God in all of His mercy came through for me and He will for you too. When I called unto Him in my deepest pit He heard my plea and came through for me. He came to me and gave me hope. Jesus loves you in spite of what you may have brought on yourself. He said if you will call upon Him He will hear and answer if you will follow Him. There is no other love such as His love for us. Even though you are serving God you can still step out of His will by letting your wants get in the way. I was saved at the age of nine and was called to do a work for God at the age of eleven. I was brought up in a Christian home and was singing gospel music with my brother and sisters with my mother playing the piano. There was no reason for me to have made such a mistake at the young age that I was but I did. I praise God that He said, He never repents of His calling. I thank Him for forgiving me and giving me another chance to do a work for Him. I can never praise Him enough. I can't change my past but I can do all I can now and in the future and give Him all of my time while I'm here on this earth. Thank God that He has allowed me to be in His permissible will. I do love Him with all of my heart.

God's plans for me was not so in the beginning. He did not plan for me to mess up in my young years. He didn't choose that for me for I made the choice myself. I have no one to blame but myself. God has given me a good Christian husband who loves the Lord with all of his heart, mind, soul and strength. God is first and I am second place in his life and that's the way God designed it. We have had a good ministry in music for about 27 years now and we both are ordained ministers. We love to preach and teach the gospel of Jesus Christ. We love the church that we are in and for six years we do the music ministry there. We still evangelize when God calls us out and we still minister in music as the Lord calls us out. We just want to please Him and do all we can for the Kingdom of God. We love to see souls saved, lives changed and bodies healed. We don't look at the denomination over the door but we go wherever God opens the doors.

I pray I have helped you as you have read this book not to make the same mistake that I did. I had to go through much un-necessary grief and sorrow because of my mistakes and I want to tell others and encourage everyone to let God have His will in your life. Seek Him for direction and choices and don't do it on your own. First of all, accept Jesus Christ as your Lord and put Him first place in your heart and life.

Jesus is coming soon to get His children in the rapture of the church so be ready. He is the groom and we are the church which is His bride. All evil will be done away with so we won't have to go through anymore sickness, pain, sorrow, grief or even death. We will live with Him forever. This was His plan in the very beginning for us to live with Him forever but sin changed that so He made another way. Jesus came, walked on this earth, teaching all men about the gospel. He died on the old rugged cross, was buried and rose again on the third day then He ascended back to Heaven with the Father, He's seated at the right hand of the Father interceding for you and me. When the Father says, Son go get My children then He will come to get all who are following Him and serving Him and who are looking and waiting for Him. Are you ready? If not, get ready while you still have time.

Chapter 8

Preparations for Blessings

*L*uke 3:4-9, Prepare ye the way for the Lord make His path straight. Every valley shall be filled and every mountain and hill shall be brought low and the crooked shall be made straight. All flesh shall see the salvation of the Lord. John the Baptist was the fore runner of Jesus Christ and he was preaching about Jesus coming. He was trying to prepare the people to see Jesus. He wanted them to be doing what was right when Jesus came. We know He came and was baptized by John in the Jordan River and many saw Him. We know He is coming again and you need to prepare to meet Him if you're not ready, get ready. Don't say I will later, for it may be too late. In order to receive the blessings from God, we have to prepare to receive. The greatest blessing and reward is to go with Him and live with Him forever. This life is the preparation time in this age we now live. After death will be too late, this life will be over and you will have made your choice and your plans where you're going after death. First of all you have to repent and accept Jesus in your heart and life and then live for Him daily. Turn from all your evil ways and from the ways of the world and turn to Him the beginning and finisher of our faith.

All the obstacles that are not pleasing to Him have to be removed from your life. You are a new person in Him now so you have to walk and talk like Him. He has already paved the way for you and you have to walk in it. Stay on the straight and narrow path. He will walk with you all of the way to your eternal home for God has called us. Many are called but few are chosen. You can't be chosen if you have not accepted His call and live for Him daily. We have to prove by the way we live that we have really turned from sin and turned to God. Just confessing it with your mouth is not good enough. Don't think that you're safe because you're a descendant of Abraham. You can't make it on someone else's faith and decision to follow Christ. Many think that because they were raised in a Christian home that it's good enough for them but you have to choose to follow Christ. Every tree that does not produce good fruit is cut down and thrown into the fire.

Things that keep you from making the right preparations

Matt.19:22, Worldly possessions kept the rich young man from following Jesus. The Bible tells us that the love of money is sin. Hardly, will a rich man enter into the Kingdom of Heaven. Verse 24, says it is easier for a camel to go through the eye of a needle than for a rich man to enter into the Kingdom of God. The reason is that rich people love their money more than the things of God and they don't want to spend it on things except what they desire. Your money is going to perish with you if you don't serve God. It is just material stuff and the only thing that will stand in the end is what you have done for God. This doesn't mean that you can't have lots of money but don't put it before Jesus Christ in your life. Don't depend on your money for it will fail you in the end. Money is not the right preparation for other blessings of God.

Luke 9:59-60, Family ties prevented a man from following Jesus. He had to rake care of his family first. You have to put Jesus first above all others and everything else. He will not be second place in your heart and life. This happens to a lot of people today and even Christians. They will stay out of church because they are having some of their family coming to visit them. When Jesus invited this man to come follow Him, he told Jesus, I have to go take care of my family first. If you will put Jesus first then Jesus will take care of your family and all else. This doesn't mean that Jesus doesn't want you to care for your family for it's your duty to care for your children and your spouse but He wants you to put Him first.

Heb.12; 1-3, Weights as well as sins slows us down or stops us from the process in the life we live for Jesus. Let us strip off every weight that so easily besets us or slows us down, especially the things that hinders us from following Jesus Christ. Let us run the race with patience and endurance, the race that God has set before us. We do this by looking unto Jesus the finisher of our faith. He is the One we depend on, He's the One who called us and He's the One who will keep us and bless us. We need to think on Him and do not grow weary or give up for we will reap the blessings of God if we faint not. Jesus endured the cross for us and all of its pain so there's nothing too hard for us that should keep us from following Him. Don't give in to the devil and his plots to make you grow weary or slow you down from serving Him and doing His will. Jesus is waiting to bless you so make the right preparations for blessings.

Warning against drifting away

Heb.2:1-4, Since all of this is true we need to pay much closer attention than ever before to the truth that we have heard unless at anytime or anyway we drift away from God. The commandments have been given to us by Moses and are proven sure. For every violation and disobedience there is a penalty. How shall we escape if we neglect and refuse to pay attention to such a great salvation? It was declared to us first by Jesus Christ our Lord and confirmed by those who personally heard Him speak. It was also established by God who showed His approval by signs and wonders and miraculous manifestations of His power and imparting the gifts of the Holy Spirit to the believers according to His own will. We need always to pay close attention to the Word of God.

Mark 14:38, Watch and pray that you will not fall into temptation, the Spirit is willing but the flesh is weak. Greater is He that is in us than he that is in the world. God the Father prepared the way for His Son Jesus Christ and Jesus prepared the way for us. God loves us with an everlasting love and has everything prepared for His children. Are we preparing the way for our children? We can't just prepare the way for ourselves but we need to be concerned for others as well, especially our children. What do they see in us? Suppose they were preparing according to what they saw in us? Would it be the right preparations? Think about it for a moment, let this sink into your heart and mind. We don't want to ever lead anyone astray from the truth of God.

How to prepare for blessings

Jesus is coming back and we believe soon. We live in this world but we can't be of it. We have to be different, we have to be a separated people to follow Jesus Christ. We have to live here until Jesus comes or we go through death, but we have to live above sin and not follow the ways of the world. We have to stay in the Word of God and pray without ceasing. We have to have a close relationship with Jesus, talk to Him. We have to stay in church, worship and praise Him at all times. You have to give of your tithes and offerings for this is the will of God for each one of us. Love your neighbor as yourself, love everyone even to your enemies and those who say all kind of evil against you and use you. We are y to help the weak and needy and stand in the gap for those in need. He said, if it be at all possible to be at peace with everyone. There are so many warnings in the Word of God for disobedience and not following God but many are not listening and taking heed to what He said. Jesus will separate the wheat from the tares, the saved from the unsaved, in the end. Now is the preparation time for blessings of God.

How much more can we tell. We have a great commission given us by the Lord Jesus Christ Himself. It's not God's will that any should perish but that all should have eternal life. We all have to prepare ourselves here and now, to be able to have the blessings of God. Then we know we will have eternal life with through Jesus Christ, forever. What are you doing to prepare? Time is running out for many. Are you ready to meet Him? Make sure you're ready and stay ready for He is coming.

I Will Make You Fishers of Men

Matt.4:18-20, Jesus called His twelve disciples. As He was walking beside the sea of Galilee He saw two brothers, Simon called Peter, and His brother Andrew. They were fishing in the lake for they were fishermen, for they fished for fish. He said unto them, come follow Me and I will make you fishers of men. They left their nets at once, and followed Jesus. These were the first disciples and they didn't ask any questions they just heeded the call and followed Jesus. They could have asked, what do you mean that You will make us fishers of men? Or, they could have said, we have a job to do and You will have to wait until we have finished it but they didn't do that, they left their job at once and followed Him. He didn't have to ask them twice or beg them. How many times do people today tell Him to wait until another time or at a more convenient time, or I'm not ready to follow You right now? Jesus is still calling disciples to come follow Him. We are His disciples if we have repented and asked Him into out hearts and lives and are living for Him daily. John 8:31, Jesus said to those Jews which believed on Him, if you continue in My Word then you are My disciple, indeed. He said, herein is My Father glorified that you bear much fruit so you shall be My disciple. To bear much fruit we must not allow anything to get in our way or hinder us from doing what God has called us to do. We have to continue to strive in His work and the biggest work is to see souls saved. We are to fish for lost souls and show them the way to Jesus. Sometimes we have to bring them to Jesus. We can't make them accept Him but we can bring them to Him. That's the job and duty of all disciples.

We have to give it all up to follow Jesus. Luke 14:33, If anyone come to Me and hate not his father, mother, wife, children, brothers and sisters, yet his own life, he cannot be My disciple. And whosoever does not pick up his cross and come after Me cannot be My disciple. This doesn't mean that we have to literally hate anyone but it means, Jesus has to be first place above all else and everyone. He will not be second over anyone or anything. We have to deny self and leave all to follow Him. We don't give anything up that He won't replace it with something better. It has been said of many that it doesn't cost anything to serve God. I beg the difference. Salvation is free to all who will accept it but we have to count the cost, the Bible teaches. Jesus gave His life for us and we have to give our life up to Him. He doesn't just want part of us but He wants our whole life, our heart, mind, soul and strength. We have a cross to bear to serve and follow Him. We have to leave family and all to follow Him. Once we come to Him we are not our own anymore for we belong to Him for we were bought with a price. We are to die to self daily. One thing for you to know and remember is, every word that ends with eth means to continue. We have to follow Him daily and with everything that is within us. Jesus said, My sheep hear My voice and I know them and they follow Me. He has called us to be fishers of men and women, boys and girls.

What we should do to see souls saved

Luke 5: 4-6, Launch out into the deep and let down your nets for an abundance. Do whatever it takes to see souls saved. Deny yourself and get out of your comfort zone. The disciples said, at Your Word Lord, I will let down the net. In other words, I will do whatever it takes to be the greatest fishers of men. When they had done what the Lord said to do, they caught a multitude of fish and their nets were not even broken. God will honor our faith, our obedience, our efforts and our diligence to follow His commands, We will see miracles happen when we follow His instruction. Our efforts are demanded of God before blessings can be given us. We are God's chosen vessels, go and endure whatever the cost to win souls and to be fishers of men. He said He would keep us from all harm and equip us with everything we need. Let your light so shine before others that they will see your good works and glorify your Father which is in Heaven.

John 15:16, You have not chosen Me but I have chosen you and ordained you that you should go out and bring forth fruit and that your fruit should remain that whatsoever you ask shall of the Father in My name, He will give it unto you. Luke 10:19, He said, I give unto you to walk on serpents and scorpions and over all the power of the enemy and nothing shall by any means hurt you. If you noticed, Jesus told His disciples to fish on the right side and you will find fish. We have to always be right in the eyes of the Lord. God has chosen you to do a work so do it with all your might. How is your fishing? Are your nets empty? When the disciples obeyed Jesus their nets were full for they caught many fish. If we would just heed to God's Word we will see souls saved. You can't fish on the wrong side and expect to see souls saved for you need to get right with God and then fish on the right side.

We can rejoice when we see souls saved

Isa.55:12, For you shall go out with joy and be led forth with peace, the mountains and hills shall break forth with singing before you and all the trees of the field shall clap their hands. All will rejoice when they see souls saved. Even the angels in Heaven rejoice over one soul that gets saved. The mountains and hills will move out of the way. The stumbling blocks has to go and move out of the way. Speak to the mountain in Jesus name and tell them to move in Jesus name. The devil will try everything he can to stop a soul from getting saved and to hinder you from fishing. We have the power in Jesus name to tell him to flee. If we draw to God then God will draw near to us and then we can flee from the devil and he will have to leave. When we turn a sinner from his evil ways then his soul is saved from hell. We can't save a sinner but we can lead them to Christ and He saves them. Our greatest desire after we come to Christ should be to see souls saved from hell. Don't ever miss an opportunity to witness to others especially to the unsaved. Don't let the blood of others be on your hands. It's always been said, you can lead a horse to the water but you can't make him drink. The same is true for a sinner, you can lead them to Christ but you can't make them accept. But when you have led them to Christ then you have done your part for Christ. We need always to pray for the lost that the Spirit of God would draw them to Christ. Prayer does change things.

The Lord's Prayer

(1) Jesus prayed for Himself,

(2) He prayed for His disciples,

(3) He prayed for the future believers

John 17: 1-5, Christ prayed for the Father to glorify Him. Jesus Christ is the greatest intercessor. He prayed, Father, the hour is come, glorify Thy Son that Your Son might glorify You. And now O Father, glorify Thou Me with Your own self with glory which I had with You before the world was. You see, Jesus was God and man. He came to earth to redeem us, His people. So now His work was done on earth and He was asking the Father to restore His place as it was in the beginning before the world was made. He was praying to restore His former glory and place. He expressed the very essential of eternal life. This is life eternal that they may know the only true God and Jesus Christ whom You have sent. I have glorified You on earth. I have finished what You gave Me to do. Jesus had done everything His Father sent Him to do and His work was finished on earth. He rejoiced in the shared glory of the Father.

Verses 6-9, Jesus prayed for His disciples. He prayed for their knowledge. He said, I have given them the Words which You gave Me and they have received them and have known that I came out from You and they have believed that You did send Me. I pray for them, I pray not for the world but for them which You have given Me for they are Yours. He prays for their perseverance. All of Yours, are Mine and Mine are Yours and I am glorified in them. And now I am no more in the world but they are in the world and I come to You. Holy Father, keep them through Your Holy name for those You gave Me that they may be one as We are One. While I was in the world I kept them in Your name, I have kept them and none of them are lost but the son of perdition that the Scripture might be fulfilled. He prayed for their joy. He said, now I come to you that they may have My joy fulfilled in themselves. Jesus prayed for their sanctification. I have given them Your Word and the world hated them because they are not of the world even as We are not of the world. I pray not that You take them out of the world but that You will keep them from evil. They are not of the world for I am not either. Sanctify them in Your truth, the Word is truth. Jesus knew that His people could not keep themselves. He knew that they would face many obstacles in this life. We can know this one thing, He is always there with us and He is interceding for us to the Father in Heaven. We could not make it through this life if it were not for Jesus Christ interceding for us.

Verses 20-26, Jesus prayed for the future believers. He prays for their oneness. He said, I don't just pray for My disciples alone but I pray for those that shall believe on Me in the future through Your Word. I pray that they may be one as You O Father and I are One. They will be one in us, that the world might believe that You have sent Me. The glory that you gave Me I have given them that they may be made perfect in one and that the world may know that You sent Me I have loved them as You have loved Me. I pray also that those that You have given Me will be with Me also. O Father, the world have not known You but I have these that You sent Me and I have declared Your name to them that the love where You have loved Me may be in them and I in them. Jesus loves His children so much that He wants to keep us in all things. There is no greater love than the love of the Father that through His Son we would be kept forever.

The mystery of godliness

I Tim.3:16, Without controversy, great is the mystery of godliness. God was manifested in the flesh, justified in the Spirit, seen of angels, preached to the Gentiles, believed on in the world and received up into glory. God made everything beautiful in it's time. He has set eternity in men's hearts yet they cannot understand or know what God had done from the beginning to end. Isaiah said, there is no searching for His understanding. Paul said, who has known the mind of God? John said, no man has seen God at anytime. The only Son which is in the bosom of the Father has declared Him. Col.1; 15, Jesus is the image of the invisible God, the first born of every creature. Jesus is the only way to become a child of God. That's through belief in Him, trusting in Him, being obedient to Him, by loving Him and living for Him. One has to believe in Jesus Christ because He's the only one who has ever seen God. There's no other way but to trust and obey Him. The just shall live by faith. Without faith you cannot please God. We have to please God and not ourselves. We are to be like Jesus and live like Him to be one of His children. You have to be born again and washed in the blood of Jesus to belong to Him. He is the way, the truth and the life and no one can come to the Father but by and through Him. Our lives have to be a living testimony by the way that we live everyday. There are a lot of mysteries in the Word of God. The Bible says, the secrets belong to God. One day we will know it all but there are things that we will never know until we get to Heaven then all things will be revealed to God's children. It's by faith and faith alone that we live and move in this Christian walk. There's been enough told that we don't have to question God for anything. He's made known to us all that we need to know. If we knew it all then we wouldn't have to live by faith, would we? This is where faith and trust comes in. We don't have to be concerned for what we don't know for God holds it all in His hands. Our future belongs to God and He will take good care of it. It is up to us to live godly, live righteous and holy unto the Lord. For without holiness we won't see God. We can't make it to Heaven without being godly, righteous and living holy. We are to live holy because Jesus is holy. Everything that we need to know is written in the Word of God.

Chapter 9

Perennial or Annual Christian

Perennial is a flower or plant that comes back and blooms each season or year. Annual is a plant or flower that you have to plant every year or season for it dies out after one planting.

Eze.47:12, By the river upon the banks thereof on this side and that side shall all trees for meat whose leaf shall not fade away neither shall the fruit thereof be consumed for it shall bring forth new fruit according to his months because the waters they shall issue out of the sanctuary and the fruit thereof shall be for meat and the leaf thereof for medicine. These trees shall never fade away or die for they shall be for food and the leaves shall be for medicine for the healing of the land. The trees shall always bear fruit. This is the way a Christian should be, alive and bear fruit. If you abide in Christ you shall live forever.

A perennial Christian is one who lives for Christ everyday and is lead by the Holy Spirit. One who doesn't fade away every time there is a problem or just live for a season. They attend the church services to be fed spiritual food so they won't fade a way or die. They are fed so they can keep their strength to bear more fruit. They are not consumed of the devil's temptations and schemes. They are given the gifts of the Spirit to be used at the proper and right time. They have the right Spirit that was issued out of the sanctuary for meat for healing. They do not fall by the wayside or fall for every wind of doctrine or teachings. They have planted their feet on the solid rock which is Jesus Christ our Lord and Savior. Their minds are made up to serve the Lord no matter what, they are sold out to Him and His works. Their roots are planted deep and they are well watered by the Holy Ghost for they look to God for their source of life and for their every need. They grow even in bad weather and storms of life. They don't let every wind of doctrine cause them to doubt or fall. Their hearts are fixed and their minds are made up to follow Christ.

Ps.92:12-14, The righteous shall flourish like the palm tree, they shall grow like the tree of Lebanon. Those that be planted in the house of the Lord shall flourish in the courts of the Lord. They shall bring forth fruit in old age, they shall be fat and flourishing. A tree grows in every season, they need every season to make them what they should be. A tree produces fruit in its season. The palm trees are strong and the trees of Lebanon are like the mighty oak, they are strong also. The perennial Christian should be strong in every season. You will have bad times as well as good times just like anyone else but you can grow strong through every trial and test like the palm trees and the trees of Lebanon. When the strong winds blow they stand strong.

The perennial Christian has constant contact with the water. Ps.1:3, They shall be like a tree planted by the rivers of water that brings forth fruit in its season. His leaf shall not wither and whatsoever they do shall prosper. They will stand strong and will not bow down to the devil and all of his tricks and schemes. Others will look upon the beauty of Jesus Christ in them. You can be strong in every trial because you have the living water keeping you flourished. He will feed you what you need when you need it in all seasons, good or bad times. Why should one weaken in trials? You are a perennial Christian, a mighty warrior for Jesus Christ. We have to follow through and endure to the end.

A perennial Christian doesn't fall in every situation. Think of yourself as the tree planted by the rivers of water. Your leaf will not wither or fade away and you will not be consumed by the tricks of the devil or of the evil ones. You will shine like the sun. You will shine when the sun isn't shinning, when things aren't going your way and when it seems like everything is falling apart. Yow will bring forth fruit that will strengthen others in their time of troubles and in their weakness. You will be a testimony and a great witness to others. Sometimes you may be the only sermon someone will see or hear.

You will bear many kinds of fruit. Gal.5:22-26, The fruit of the Spirit is, love, joy, peace, long sufferings, gentleness, goodness, faith and temperance. Against such things there is no law. There is no law that says we can't have these gifts of the Spirit. If you will notice, there is only one fruit, the fruit of the Spirit but there are many gifts. When we live God's way, He brings good gifts in our lives, things like affection for others. We develop a willingness to stick with the things of God, a sense of compassion in the heart and a conviction of holiness in our life. We find ourselves involved in commitments, not needing to force our way in life but to lean on the Lord. We will want to do the things of the Lord for that will be our greatest desire, to please the Lord in everyway. We won't feel we have to force or pushed to please God for we will know that, we were born to serve the Lord. We don't have to serve Him because we have to but because we want to. We will be like this because we have learned to crucify our flesh of all fleshly lusts. If we live in the Spirit then let us walk in the Spirit also. Let us not be desirous of vain glory, provoking one another or envying one another. Give God all of the glory and praise for what He's doing in your life and how He's using you for His Kingdom. Never misuse the gifts that He's given you.

God has chosen you

John 15:16, Jesus said, You have not chosen Me, but I have chosen you and ordained you that you should go forth and bring forth fruit and that your fruit should remain that whatsoever you ask of the Father in My name He may give it to you. You are now filled with the fruit of righteousness which is by Jesus Christ unto the glory and praise of God. Paul said, I desire fruit that will abound to your account. He is saying here, don't go back to your old ways or you will lose out, you will fade away, you must endure to the end. Walk worthy of the Lord being all pleasing to Him. Be fruitful in every good works and increasing in the knowledge of God. Many are called but few are chosen. It's not God's will that any should perish but that all would have eternal life. Some will not accept the call of God. Praise God that He has chosen you and you have heeded the call. Never take any credit for who you are in the Lord, give Him all the glory and praise for where He brought you from and for keeping you in His loving care. You belong to Him for you were bought with a great price. You are not your own anymore to do what you want but to do what is pleasing to Him. We have to abide in Christ Jesus to the end. He that endures to the end, the same shall be saved.

The annual Christian or carnal Christian

Matt.13:4-7, But others fell by the wayside and the fowls came and ate them up. Some fell on stony places, they grew lanky. The sun burned them and they were scorched, they withered away and died. Some fell on thorns and were choked out. Seeds can only grow on good ground. Some fell because of the hardness of their hearts and by careless hearing and they allowed the devil to put them through the mill, so to speak. They weren't listening to what the Lord was saying to them and listening to the devil. Those that fell on stony places were the emotional hearers those that live shallow lives. They had physical limitations of the flesh. They let the flesh control them and not the Spirit of God. Those that fell on thorns are the ones who have worldly cares, other things that are more important than putting God first. Jesus said, Seek first the Kingdom and His righteousness then all of these other things will be added unto you.

Luke 10:41-42, Jesus told Martha, You have many cares and are troubled about many things. Jesus told her, one thing you lack and is needed and Mary has chosen that part which shall not be taken away from her. Mary chose to take the time with Jesus instead of doing other things while Martha felt she needed to be doing other things. Some Christians that are called by His name make all kind of excuses for not going to God's house to worship Him. Sometimes it would be a headache, or they went to bed late on Sat. night so they have to rest on Sun. morning. For some, it's bad weather, a little rain or a little uncomfortable and they want to stay in their comfort zone. Jesus will not be second place to any one or anything. He won't take what's left over for He wants all of you. We are no one's judge but Jesus knows your heart and mine and He knows if we are sold out completely to Him. There's no time for playing church but it is a serious matter, it's a matter of life and death. I really don't know how one can be an annual Christian for Jesus said, you are either for Me or against Me. You can't be a part time Christian. You can't be on and off and be a child of God. Jesus tells us this many times in His Word.

Matt.3; 10, The ax is already laid unto the root of the tree. Therefore, every tree which does not bear fruit is cut down and cast into the fire to be burned. There is coming a divine judgment for unfruitfulness. Gal.5:19-21, tells us about the works of the flesh. I tell you as I have told you before in time past, that they which do such things shall not enter into the Kingdom of Heaven, idolatry, sorcery, strife, selfishness, dissensions, immorality, impurity, anger, envy, drunkenness, and carousing and the like. If anyone does these things they will not enter into the Kingdom of Heaven. Joshua said, choose ye this day whom you will serve. Jesus said in Revelation, if you are lukewarm I will spew you out of My mouth. You are either for Him or against Him. There is no such thing as straddling the fence as some have said. You're either on one side or the other. It's a fearful thing to fall into the hands of the living God. You can't be of the world and be a child of God. We live in this world but true Christians are not of the world. We are a separated people, a peculiar people set apart from the world.

I Thess.5; 23, And the God of peace sanctify you wholly and I pray God your whole Spirit, soul and body be preserved unto the coming of our Lord Jesus Christ. Keep the commandment without spot, unto the coming of the Lord. God's Word is to be kept sacred, the entire Word and not just in part. All He has asked is that we be faithful and obedient to Him.

A perennial Christian has their hearts and minds set on the things of God. Their hearts are fixed as David said. A perennial Christian will keep God's Word and please Him. What are you? Is your mind made up to serve Him and Him alone? Jesus is coming, be ready and don't be left behind. He is coming for those who are ready, who are watching and waiting for Him. He's coming for a bride who is without spot, blemish or wrinkle. We live in His righteousness because our righteousness is as filthy rags. There's nothing good in us but Jesus Christ. The only things that will last is what we do for Him and the Kingdom of God.

The greatest healthy growth is Spiritual life

II Pet.1:2-11, Simon Peter a servant and an apostle of Jesus Christ to those through the righteousness of God and Savior Jesus Christ have received a faith as precious as ours. Grace and peace be yours in abundance through the knowledge of God and of Jesus Christ our Lord. Peter is writing to those whose experience with God is life changing and all is due to the glory of God and Savior Jesus Christ. For He gets all of the glory for our salvation.

God has called us to a Spiritual life. His divine power has given us everything we need for life and godliness through the knowledge of Him who has called us by His glory and goodness. Everything that has been given us goes into a life pleasing to Him by getting to know Him personally and intimately. That's the best invitation we've ever had. That God He has called us and is living within us. If you have accepted Him into your heart and life then He is living within your heart. God is so big yet He can live within us, which is a real miracle in itself. Praise God for such great love for us.

We are secured by His precious promises. Through these He has given us His very great and precious promises so that through them you may participate in the divine nature and escape the corruption in the world caused by evil desires. Jesus paid the price for our ticket for salvation to walk in the life of God and to turn our backs on the world of lust and sin.

Eight essential steps in the development and fruitfulness

1- Faith, 2- Goodness, 3- Knowledge, 4- Self control, 5- Perseverance, 6- Godliness, 7- Brotherly kindness and 8- Love. Verse 5, For every reason make every effort to add to your faith, goodness, knowledge, self control, perseverance, godliness, brotherly kindness and love. For if anyone possess these qualities in increasing measure they will keep you from being ineffective, unproductive, idle or unfruitful in your knowledge of our Lord Jesus Christ. If anyone does not have these qualities then they are blind or near sighted and have forgotten that they have been cleansed from their past sins. These qualities lead to Holiness and without holiness you won't see God and you cannot please Him. He is holy so we have to be holy. All of these steps are very essential to live a Christian life that is fulfilling to each Christian and pleasing to God the Father.

Our final destiny

Verse 10, Finally, my brethren, be all the more eager to make your calling sure and elections sure. For if you do these things, then you will never fall. You will receive a rich welcome into the Kingdom of Heaven of our Lord and Savior Jesus Christ. God's invitation is to all who will accept and live for Him. This is the greatest invitation one could ever get. If you will do what He says then you will have a life here on a firm footing. Some people believe that once saved you can never fall. The Word tells us here that if we keep these things we will never fall. You can't live any ole way and do things that God has opposed of and stay saved. He said, if you will do these things you will never fall. If it weren't possible to fall then He would have not told us this. He said in verse 10; make sure of your calling and election. We are to make sure that we elect to do what's right in God's sight and then He will provide the entry into the kingdom of Heaven. If you don't keep these qualities of God, what makes you any difference than the world?

We can't even imagine the beauty that God has in store for us. Streets of gold and the way open into life eternal with the Master and Savior Jesus Christ. We can have life more abundantly here for He has promised His children this. He said that it was His will that we prospered and be in good health just as our souls prospered. That's the secret, prosper as our soul prospers. We have to feed our Spirit and keep ourselves tuned into God for our soul to prosper. We have to die to self daily and live for God, doing the things that please Him. This is the way we can have healthy growth and have the greatest Spiritual life here and have eternal life later, forever. Keep the fire burning and our lights on so everyone can see Jesus in you. God has called us into this Spiritual life and we are secured by His promises as long as we follow Him. He said He would never leave or forsake us and He would be with all the way and we can depend on that. We are to live everyday like it's the last one and enjoy every moment in the Lord. God wants us to enjoy life here while we prepare for the next life. There is no better life than living it in Jesus.

What are you made of?

Are you weak when trials and troubles come your way? Are you weak spiritually? Trials will let you know what you're made of and how strong you really are. Do you faint under pressure? Who do you call on when you have problems? Do you lose your joy under pressure and problems of this life? Can others see Jesus in you when you're going through troubles? Are you walking in the flesh or are you walking by the Spirit of God? Who is in control of your life, you or the Lord Jesus Christ?

John 16:12, Jesus said, I have many things to tell you but you cannot bear them because you are weak in the flesh. I Cor.3:1-3, Paul said, I could not talk to you as spiritual but as unspiritual because you are of the flesh and you are letting the carnal nature predominate you. You are like an infant and I have to feed you with milk and not solid food… You are not strong enough and ready for strong meat. You are unspiritual and letting the flesh control you. For as long as you have envy, jealousy, and friction among you then you are still walking in the flesh and doing what pleases the flesh. You are still like an unchanged person and not of Christ. A jealous, envious and contrary heart never pleases God. There are still lots of people in the churches that causes divisions and strife and God is not pleased with them. Many are jealous and are envious of other Christians. Many have a spirit of control. We still have a lot of people who are called by Jesus name but are not spiritual. The natural person doesn't understand the Spiritual person or spiritual things. That's why there is so much division in the churches. If everyone was of the same Spirit then all would understand each other in the Lord. That's why you should never appoint someone in a position in God's work that's not spiritual. They can't understand the Spiritual things of God.

Let's consider Job for a moment. He was perfect and upright, feared God and shunned evil. He has seven sons and three daughters. He was a rich man but he loved God more than anything else in the world. His children sinned and enjoyed the things of the world but Job prayed for them early in the morning and offered burnt offering to God for them. He was afraid they had cursed God in their hearts so he stood in the gap for them. God allowed the devil to do anything to him that he wanted to do except to touch him. He lost all of his children and smote the house that the children were in and the house fell on them and all died. In all of these things Job did not sin. He said, the Lord gives and the Lord takes away, blessed be the Name of the Lord. Job is a prime example for the children of God. Job knew that God was in control so he didn't grumble or complain. He did get angry but God said we can be angry and sin not. Job rose up and tore his clothes, shaved his head and fell on his knees on the ground and worshipped the Lord. In his anger he worshipped the Lord. How many times do you do that in your anger? He was grieved and in sorrow but he had submitted his life to God and he knew he was in God's hands. Job's life didn't end here for he had many more problems. He was smote with boils from the sole of his feet to the top of his head. Now I know how just one boil feels but I can't imagine all over your body. His wife told him to curse God and die and Job told her she talked like a foolish woman. Should we accept the good things from the Lord and not the bad as well? In all of this Job did not sin. You will find this in the third chapter of Job. He was weary of life I'm sure for he was troubled and oppressed for a season. He told his friend that man was born into troubles but that he had sought God and unto Him he committed his cause.

God does great things without number. Happy is the one who God correct. Don't despise the chastising of the Lord God for He is Almighty. He said, happy is the one God corrects. He will deliver you out of troubles Are you happy when God corrects you? He does it because He loves you. Job was weary of life but he told God, you know I am not wicked or evil and there is none that can take me out of Your hand. He told God, even if You slay me yet, I will trust You. I will maintain my ways before You. Job said in 14:1, I knew that man was born of woman for a few days and it would be full of troubles. But he knew God was going to take care of him through it all.

We were never promised all good days. But we were promised that all who followed Christ would have trials and tribulations all the days of our life her, but He also promised that He would make a way for us and go with us all of the way. Draw near to God and He will draw near to you. Jesus faced many obstacles in this life here too. The devil tried to tempt Him in the wilderness for 40 days and nights but He never gave in to him or sinned. He was strong and firm in the Father. We can stand strong in Jesus through our problems too. He is our strength in our weakness and He is strong through us. Job said, I know that my Redeemer lives, even though my body is destroyed I will see God. He had a Heavenly vision from God and He trust Him all of the way. He knew that God knew the way that He took and when God had tried him that he was going to come through like gold tried in the fire. 42:12, Through all of the sufferings and trials the Lord blessed Job and his latter end was much better than the first and he died at an old age. He lived 140 years after God had blessed him.

Things that make you stronger when troubles come your way

(1) If you will transform your mind God will transform your life.

(2) Don't worry about things that you can't change

(3) What you say in the midst of your trials has a great impact on how long you will stay in the midst of it.

(4) If you will change your and start trusting Him.

(6) Trust God when life doesn't make sense.

(7) Stop talking about how big your problem is and start talking about how big God is.

Job 42:2, We have to believe as Job did. I know You can do everything and there is no thought that can be withheld from Him. Matt.19:26, Jesus said unto them, with men this is impossible but with God all things are possible. For with God nothing is impossible. Whatever problems we may go through, God can fix them. We can't but He can. We have trials so we can grow strong and worship God in the good times and in bad times and see if He won't bless you and bring you out of your bondage.

II Cor.12:9. My grace is sufficient for you for My strength is made strong in your weakness. Paul said, I'd rather glory in my infirmities so that the power of God can rest upon me. I take pleasure in infirmities, reproaches, necessities, persecutions, infirmities and in distresses for Christ sake. We need to learn to lean on Him at all times through the good and the bad. He is our strength, our hope, our salvation, our healer and all that we need. David said, the Lord is my strength and my Shield. My heart trust in Him and I am helped therefore my heart greatly rejoices and with my song I will praise Him all the time. The Lord gives strength to His people and He will bless them with peace. Wait on the Lord and be of good courage and He will strengthen your heart. Wait, I say, wait on the Lord. We can tell what a person is made of in their actions, when they are going through the problems of life. The joy of the Lord is your strength and it will show in your actions.

Rom.8:28, For we know that all things work together for the good of those who love the Lord and are called according to His purpose. We do not understand why some things happen but we do know this one thing. If you are a child of God, you can trust Him in whatever's going on in your life. He has a plan and purpose for each and every child of His and He is in control. What are you made of? God made you in the image of Himself and He has called you to serve Him. You now have the Holy Spirit dwelling in you so let Him lead and guide you all of the way in everything you do and everywhere you go and what you say. You are made up of the body, soul and spirit. Don't let your body control you but let the Spirit of God control you, then you will be of God. You are God's child so act like it. Remember, the natural person is different from the person who is lead by God. Stay strong in the Lord, think positive, speak positive and live holy.

You are what you eat

We're going to talk about Spiritual food you eat and the natural foods. We live in the natural body for we have not yet been changed from this mortal body to the immortal body that we'll have when we get to Heaven. But we have to walk in the Spiritual realm to make it to Heaven. We came into this world a sinner but we can't stay a sinner in order to enter the Kingdom of Heaven. There has to be a change in us. All have to be born again and washed in the blood of Jesus Christ.

John 6;53-54, Jesus said unto them, Verily, verily I say unto you, except you eat the flesh of the Son of man and drink His blood you have no life in you. Who ever eats My flesh and drink My blood has eternal life and I will raise them up at the last day. Jesus was saying, truly I say to you, there is only life in My flesh and My blood. You may exist in this world without Me but there is no life without Me. I came into this world and ate of My Father and you have to eat of Me to have eternal life and have it more abundantly here on this earth. Just as a new born baby desires the milk to grow we should be hungry for the Word of God. When you have tasted the Word then you know that it is good and you want more just like you do when you taste real food and it's good then you want more. Jesus told the devil when he was being tempted by him, you can't live on bread alone but by every Word that comes out of the mouth of God. We have to be fed spiritually as well as natural food. Spiritually food comes from God in Heaven. He knows just what we need and He feeds His children.

David said, how sweet Thy Word is unto my taste, yes, sweeter than the honey in my mouth. Jeremiah said, Your Words were found and I did eat them and they were to me joy and refreshing to my heart for I am called by Your name O Lord of hosts. When we keep the Word of God in our hearts and lives and we have problems we will show forth what we really are. We will show forth what we eat. If we eat of the things of the devil and of the world then we will act like the devil and the world. If we eat of the Word of God then we will act godly and like Christ. We will definitely show forth what we eat and what we are.

Spiritual food

Isa.55:2, Hearken unto me and eat what is good and let your soul delight itself in fatness. Let your soul grow fat and not your flesh parts. If we spent as much time feeding our soul as we do our flesh then our soul would be more healthy and strong. We can't expect to read just a few lines in the Word of God everyday and expect to grow spiritually. In order to fight the devil and his evil forces we have to eat the Word of God everyday, don't just read but study His Word. Keep it in your heart and on your mind. Jesus said He is the living Word that came down from Heaven. If anyone eats of this bread they shall live forever. He gave His life for the life of the world. He doesn't want anyone to perish but all to have eternal life. The Word of God is food for out souls. We can survive with the natural foods but we will never survive without the Spiritual food from God. Luke 6:21, Blessed are they that hunger and thirst now for they shall be filled. Seek Him now while He may be found. God will fill you if you are desiring Him. If you are thirsty and dry come to the Living Water which is Jesus Christ. Ps.36; 8, They shall be filled with the fatness of Thy house. What house? There are benefits in God's house. God moves among His people and they are blessed. The sweet communion we have with God's people is wonderful. We are completely satisfied with the Spiritual food that He feeds us. We have comfort, peace and complete satisfaction. The Lord satisfies your mouth with good things. Our body is the temple of the Lord so He lives within us and He will satisfy us with the fatness of His Spirit. He said that you can have the desires of your heart when you follow Me. God wants us to be fulfilled with His goodness.

He will satisfy the longing of your soul and He will fill the hungry soul with gladness. The Lord gives food to all flesh and His mercy endures forever. The Lord shall satisfy your soul in drought and make your bones fat. In Revelation Jesus said, they will no longer be hungry or thirsty anymore. For the Lamb which is in the midst of the throne shall feed them. These are the ones that have made it through and are now living in the Kingdom of God. Praise the Lord.

How much of God do you want? How hungry or thirsty are you? You can have all you want of God. He will not give you anymore than what you can digest at one time. So the more you grow the more He will give you. We can have all we want. Please don't stay on the milk but grow in the Lord so He can feed you on the meat of the Word.

Our bodies are what we eat also in the natural. Certain foods go against our health. Our bodies are the temple of the Lord so we are to eat healthy food for our body to stay healthy and strong in the natural. So spiritually and naturally we are what we eat. If we eat too much in the natural then we are over weight, unhealthy and it causes lots of problems. We may not stop all sickness but we can prevent some. In 2009 there was a research on diets and it was said that obesity was on the rise and was causing a lot of health problems such as, diabetes, strokes, heart attacks, changes in the brain chemistry, disrupts your sleep habits, slows down your thinking and other behaviors. You know, the brain is the foundation of all behavior, including eating. So you see, we have to be careful of what we eat because it affects our natural body. God wants His children to be healthy and strong in body as well as spiritually. To grow strong in our bodies we have to eat right. To grow strong in our spirit we have to stay in tuned with God and do the things that pleases Him and stay in His Word and be obedient to it.

Chapter 10

We Can Do All Things through Christ Jesus

Phil.4:13, I can do all things through Christ Jesus who gives me strength. We can do nothing of ourselves for we are weak but He is strong and when we are weak then we are strong in Him. We need to learn to trust Him in all things. Don't ever say, I can't do this or that because we can do all things through Jesus. There's nothing too big for Him and too little that He doesn't care about. Just let go and let God for He never fails or never messes up and He's always on time and is never late as we think sometimes. If anything is messed up, we do it. So many times we want something from God or help from Him but we tell Him what to do and how to do it. He doesn't need our help for He knows what to do in every situation. We will make it to a place of success in Jesus if we let Him take control. He's our leader, keeper, driver, insurance and our engine. He's our driver, our pilot not our co-pilot. Paul said, I have learned to be content in any situation. I know what it is to be in need and I know what it is to have plenty. I have learned the secret of being content in any and every situation whether well fed in hunger or living in plenty. Now if you rebel and refuse to let Jesus help you then you will be in trouble, because your way is not His way.

Works and ways of the devil are temptations, trials and all kind of problems, pain and sorrows. The ways to success is not a straight road all of the way. Here are some things that will trip you and me up at times. Jesus never said the way to Heaven would be an easy one or that we wouldn't have any troubles but He did say that if you follow Me you would have trials and tribulations all the days of your life. But it will be worth it when we see Jesus. Heaven will surely be worth it all.

(1) There are many <u>curves</u> in the road on this Christian walk, called failures. We do fail many times but we don't quit, we just get up start over again and with Jesus help we make it.

(2) There are <u>loops</u> called confusion. Sometimes we don't know what way to turn. We think we know the right way but it seems to be wrong. Things look right but again they seem to be wrong. We have to make decisions but can't seem to make the right one. That's when we really have to trust in Jesus for He will lead you in the right direction and will give you complete peace about it.

(3) There are <u>speed bumps</u> called friends. Friends will let you down and many times hurt. Jesus said to trust no man, meaning no one. We will go through much hurt when friends let you down or speak about you in a negative way to others. There are times when you have said things in secret to friends and then they told it to someone else and it got back to you. There's a hurt that seem never to go away and it won't unless you turn it over to Jesus and let Him handle it.

(4) There <u>red lights</u> called enemies. Jesus had enemies and He still does so we can rest assure that we as Christians will also. Some of whom we think are friends are really our enemies. Our enemies are from the devil if they go against what we are doing for the Lord. Many will go against you when you are standing strong for the Lord. You can really know who are of the Lord and who aren't by the way they do and act. Jesus said to separate yourselves from these kinds of people.

(5) There are <u>caution lights</u> called family. Many times your very own family and kin will turn against you. Jesus said that He didn't come to cause peace but to cause separation and a sword. When you are serving the Lord and your family is not then it will cause a separation between you and them. You don't have anything in common with them because they are living by the world's standards and you are living by God's standards. They will many times make fun of you or be judgmental of you. This really hurts but look at the people that has turned their backs on Jesus and they will do the same to Christians.

(6) You will have <u>flats</u> called jobs. Many lave lost their jobs and can't seem to find another one. Many of these are Christians and it affects the

whole family. Many have even lost their homes because of no jobs. Stay in the Lord for many times He has a better job waiting for you. Don't give up as long as you are in Christ He will make a way for you because He said He would. Trust Him for He cares for you. He is your strength, hope, salvation, keeper and assurance. Continue to love Him and have faith in Him. He will not let you down for He said He would never leave or forsake you and you can rest in that. He will give you peace through everything if you stay in Him and trust Him.

Remember what Paul said, I can do all things through Jesus Christ who strengthen me. Be content in every situation and wait upon the Lord. Put it all into His hands and let Him lead you. He can fix all things for His children. He knows just what you need and when you need it. If you are in Jesus Christ then He has theses things for you.

(1) There is a spare called determination. If you are determined to follow Jesus then He has another way for you. He will always make a way for you where there seem to be none. We need to be like David said, my heart is fixed. He had a made up heart and mind to serve God and that's what it takes today. We have to be determined to serve and follow Jesus no matter what goes on with us or around us.

(2) There is an engine called perseverance. We have to persevere and not quit when we go through hard times. He that endures to the end will be saved. We can't start this walk with Jesus and then quit when we go through hard places in our life. Don't let your engine quit and if it slows down push even harder to persevere in Jesus. We can do all things through Jesus Christ who gives us strength.

(3) We have insurance called faith. We cannot please God without faith. The just shall live by faith. Faith is the substance of things not seen but the evidence of things hoped for. We've never seen Jesus but we have faith that one day we will. There are too many prophesies that has come to pass in the Word of God that we can know that He is real and all the things that He said He will do. You have this insurance if you have been born again and walking in Him that you will be saved if you endure to the end.

(4) We have a driver called Jesus Christ. He knows the way and He knows how to take you around the curves, loops and bumps in this life.

He made the way for us and He's been down this road before us. He is a safe and careful driver. Even in death we are safe for He is still driving and we are in His complete care. We will never be lost as long as we trust and obey Him.

(5) We have a <u>keeper</u> called Jesus. He is the One who will keep you from falling. He's the One who keeps your salvation for you can't keep it yourself. He will keep us through the good times and the bad times. Always remember, He's our pilot not our co-pilot for He is in charge of our life as long as we let Him. He doesn't force anyone to do anything for all are free to choose. Don't be foolish and do things your way. Let Jesus lead you for He has a plan for you. He will keep you through all things.

Living for God

I Pet.4:1-16, Since Jesus suffered in His body then arm yourselves with the same attitude. He had to be ready to suffer too. For if you are willing to suffer for Christ then you have decided to stop sinning. As a result you don't spend your life here on earth for earthly desires but rather the will of God. You have spent enough time in the past doing what godless people do sinfully, lust, feasting, drunkenness and wild parties. You can't change the past but you can start today living for God. A life living for God is rewarding here and then life forever with Him. You have nothing to lose and everything to gain. The same crowd that you once ran with will think it is strange of you when you don't join them in the wicked things they do and they will say evil or bad things about you. They will even make fun of you and laugh at you so don't be surprised if you have to change your friends. They will have to face God who will judge everyone, both the living and the dead. The end to all things is near therefore, be clear minded and self controlled. Be earnest in all your prayers. Most important of all, show love for each other for love covers a multitude of sins. When you start living for God and doing His will, your life has to change completely. You will not want to do the same things you once did or go places you once did or even go with the same friends. Your desire will be to please the Lord your God. This is real happiness and joy. Your thoughts will even change. You will have love like never before for everyone. You are now living and not just existing for you are a changed person.

Suffering for being a Christian

Verses 12-16, Don't be surprised at the fiery trials you are going through as if something strange was happening to you. But rejoice that you are partakers of Christ's sufferings and when His glory shall be revealed you may be glad with exceeding joy. If you be insulted for being a Christian, be happy for then the Spirit of God will come upon you. If you suffer, let it not be for wrong doings like, murder, stealing, making trouble or a busy body in other people's business, lying, adultery, slander or any other sin. If you suffer, let it be for being a follower of Jesus Christ. Never be ashamed of Jesus or for being a Christian but always praise God that you bear His name. Be led by the Spirit of God and don't let your flesh be in control of you. The biggest battle you will face will be your flesh against the Spirit. The Holy Spirit is living within you and you have the power to overcome the flesh.

I Pet.5:8-11, Be careful, be self controlled. Watch out for the attacks from the devil who is your enemy. He goes around seeking whom he may devour. He acts like a lion but he's not. Take a firm stand against him and be strong in your faith in God. All Christians all over the world are going through problems of some sort so you're not alone. The God of grace has called you unto His eternal glory by His Son Jesus Christ. After you have suffered a while He'll make you perfect, restore you and make you strong, firm and steadfast. To Him be all glory and power forever. Amen. We give all of the praise and glory to God the Father and Creator of all the universe.

Remember this also

I Cor.10:13, No temptation is come upon you except what is common to man. He will not let you be tempted above what you can bear. When you are tempted He will provide a way out so you can stand up under it. He will never leave or forsake you because He cares for you. He will carry your burdens and lighten your loads. He said to cast all of your burden upon Him for He cares for you. Submit yourselves to God, draw near to Him and He will draw near to you. Resist the devil and he will flee from you. God knows your every thought, your actions and all about you. Trust Him in all things and lean not upon your own understanding and He will direct your path.

Greater is He that is within you than he that is in the world. There is a battle at hand, there's no question about it. But there is power for there's victory in Jesus Christ our Lord and Savior. Jesus has told us that we would have problems but He will be right there with us. He is a very present help in time of troubles. Jesus is the way, the truth and the light and no one can come to the Father except through Him. He is the way maker and our keeper. We are winners with Him for He is our strength, salvation healer, comforter and our peace. He is our everything.

Fasting, praying and praising

Fasting means self sacrifice. We have to die to self to be able to fast for Christ. We have to give up something of the flesh. There are things that won't come out or be delivered of without fasting and prayer together. Joel 2:12-15, Therefore says the Lord, turn to Me with all your heart with fasting, weeping and mourning. Sanctify a fast, call a solemn assembly, gather the elders and all the inhabitants of the land and as a destruction from the Almighty shall it come. God has tried to prepare His children for what is coming that's why He has told us not only to pray but to fast also. We need to sacrifice ourselves to Him. There is power in fasting. When we deny ourselves and turn to God completely with our whole heart and life, He comes in and gives us strength and the power of the Holy Spirit works within us.

Mark 9; 29, Jesus healed the demonic man. The disciples ask Him, why couldn't they cast out the demons from him and Jesus told them, this kind comes out by prayer and fasting. Matt.6:16-17, Jesus told us how our appearance should be when we fast. He said when you fast don't look sad but wash your face and anoint your head. Be clean, be happy and rejoice for your Father in Heaven hears and He will reward you. Meaning, He will answer your prayers and will honor your fasting. Jesus fasted 40 days and 40 nights when He was in the wilderness being tempted of the devil. So did Moses. Many fasted 3 days and 3 nights and we need to fast more today than we do for we are going through many difficult trials and problems. We are living in the last days on earth as we know it. There are still many lost souls and many hurting Christians that we need to lift up to God. It will take fasting along with prayer as Jesus has taught us. How serious are you in seeing God move in situations?

Not only do we give up food but we may have to give up other things for a while as well. A lot of Christians give up TV or doing something that they really enjoy for a while to fast and pray. However God leads you then that's how you should fast. There is power in fasting and there is peace as well.

We should always pray in Jesus Name. John 14:13, Whatever you ask in My name, I will do it that the Father in Heaven may be glorified. Many prayers are not answered because they have not been prayed in Jesus name. All things are done in the name of Jesus. Many times we miss out on the blessings of God because we don't do it in His name or in His will or way. John 16:23-24, Jesus told His disciples, before now, you have not asked anything in My name. Ask and you shall receive that your joy may be full. He told them they could go directly to the Father when they ask in His name and He would grant them their request because they ask in Jesus name. Jesus was preparing them because He knew that He was going to leave them and go to the Father in Heaven. This was being for His children today and for all the generations to come. When you don't pray in Jesus name then you are praying amiss and your prayers won't be answered. Can you imagine how many prayers are never answered because of not asking in Jesus name? I still hear some pray and never say, in Jesus name. Many don't even know this or I believe that they would always pray in the name of Jesus. That's why you should study the Word of God so you will learn all these truths of God.

Jesus said to pray in the Spirit. This will cause a lot of controversy because not all understand about the Holy Spirit. Epe.6:18, Praying always with all prayer and supplication in the Spirit. There's power in the Spirit. Rom.8:26, The Spirit helps our infirmities for we don't know what to pray for as we should but the Spirit itself makes intercessions for us with groaning which cannot be uttered. And He searches the heart knowing what the mind of the Spirit is because He makes intercessions for the saints according to the will of God. You don't know what you are praying when the Spirit prays to God through you. Neither does the devil know what the Spirit is praying so he can't hinder the prayers. The Holy Spirit knows what you need and He prays to God for you and me. There is power in the name of Jesus and there is power in the Holy Ghost.

We are to pray without ceasing. The effectual prayer of a righteous person avails much. They have deep feelings and compassions for what they are praying for. They have a burning desire to pray and not faint.

Jesus told His disciples to pray and not faint. He was saying, do not give up, and don't quit asking, seeking and knocking. Hold on until your answer comes through for you. Be persistent in your praying. He may tell you to wait a while for your answer, He may say no or He may give you what you ask for right away. Whichever the case be patient without complaining.

Believe what you pray for that it will come to pass. Matt.21:21-22, If you have faith and not doubt all things whatever you ask (in My name) believe and you shall have them. You can say to your mountain, move in the name of Jesus and it shall move in the deepest sea. James 1:6, Let them ask in faith nothing wavering, for they that doubt is like the wave of the sea, tossed and driven with waves and winds, tossed everywhere. Jesus said, If you can believe all things are possible to them that believe.

We have to abide in Christ Jesus. John 15:7 and 10, Ask and it shall be done unto you. If you keep My commandments you shall abide in My love even as I have kept My Father's commandments and abide in His love. If you say you abide in Him then you shall walk as He walked. Whoever abides in Him does not sin. Just saying that you abide in Christ is not enough for you have to live it and walk it everyday. If God is not answering your prayers then I suggest you check out yourself to see if you are following through with what He has said. He doesn't always give us everything we ask for because some things wouldn't be good for us at the time we ask for them. We need to always ask His will be done. If we ask anything against His will then we won't receive it. We should never desire anything that's not of His will for us. We are to desire His will be done in our lives.

We have to be in agreement. If two of you on earth agree as touching anything, you shall ask and it will be done for them of My Father which is in Heaven. I Cor.1:10, I beg of you all to speak the same thing let there be no division among you, and be perfectly joined together in the same mind, Be in one accord. God will not work where there is division or disagreements. Just look at the upper room where there were 120 in the room in one accord and they were all filled with the Holy Ghost. Division causes confusion and confusion is of the devil. So when two or more of you are praying and seeking God be sure to be in agreement and in one accord to get your prayers answered.

Sin will keep your prayers from being answered. II Chr.7; 14, If My people who are called by My name will humble themselves, pray, seek My face and turn from their wicked ways then I will hear from Heaven and will forgive them of their sins and heal their land. Let no sin reign in your body. Ps.66:18, If I regard or hide iniquity in my heart, the Lord will not hear me. You see, God knows everything. You may hide things from others but you can't hide anything from God because He sees everything. Sin will separate you and your prayers from God. He does not look upon sin and hear your prayer.

Disobedience and despising the laws of God will hinder your prayers. Prov.1:24 and 28, If a person shuts his ears to the cry of the Lord, he will cry out and not be answered. They shall call upon Me and I will not answer. God knows His children and He knows you by name. Isa.59:2, Sin separates our prayer from being heard and answered. But your sins have separated between you and your God and your sins has hid His face from you that He will not hear. Prov.28:9, The prayers of a person who ignores the law are despised by God. If anyone turns a deaf ear to the law even their prayers are hated. We are to keep all of His commandments and laws. By this we know we are the children of God when we love Him we will keep His commandments.

If we neglect the mercy for others it will hinder our prayers. Prov.21:13, If a person shuts up the cry of the poor, he will cry out and will not be heard or answered. Blessed are the merciful for they shall obtain mercy. If you want mercy then you have to give mercy. If we don't forgive others then God won't forgive us either. We are to feel what each other is going through and have mercy not judgment or condemnation for them. Have mercy on others, pray and fast for them.

We are to praise and give thanks to God always. Epe.5:20, Giving thanks always for all things unto God and the Father in the name of our Lord and Savior Jesus Christ. In everything give thanks for this is the will of God in Christ Jesus concerning you. In everything in prayer and supplication with thanksgiving let your request be known to God. It is a good thing to give thanks unto the Lord and to sing praises unto Thy name O Most High. Offer unto God thanksgiving and pay vows unto the Most High. Lets be as David, I will greatly praise the Lord with my whole heart and with my mouth and when I am alone or in the assembly and the multitude of the upright in the congregation. For He is worthy to be praised. There is none other but God the Father, the Son and the Holy Spirit to be praised. The three are one and is worthy to be praised. Praise Him in all things.

Ps.66:20, Blessed be God which has not turned away my prayers nor His mercy from me. Isaiah 59:1, The Lord's hand is not shortened that it can't save neither His ear heavy that He cannot hear. We need to praise God so much more than we do because He has done so much for us. He's always there waiting to hear from His children. He wants to meet all of our needs and give us the desire of our hearts. God is good all of the time. He never fails us and when we fail Him He still loves us and forgives us when we ask. I praise God for forgiving me and keeping me in His care all of these years. My desire is to serve Him all of the days of my life and to live with Him forever in His Kingdom. I will not forget that I can do all things through our Lord Jesus Christ. All things are possible through Him.

Chapter 11

God Takes care of His Children Forever

*J*esus said. If you abide in Me then I will abide in you forever. He said, I will never leave or forsake My children. In order for you to be His child you have to be born again. Then you have to follow Him, be obedient to Him and trust Him with all of your heart, mind, soul and strength. No one can pluck you out of His hand but you can turn away from Him and forsake His ways. Many Christians believe in eternal security once you are born again but you have eternal security as long as you are following Jesus and are one of His children. You can fall away because of willful sin. He who knows to do good and does it not to them it is sin. You have to be obedient and faithful to God. You can't live as you please but you have to please Him who laid down His life for you which is Jesus Christ.

Ps.121:1-8, I will lift up my eyes to the hills where my help comes from. My help comes from the Lord the maker of Heaven and earth. He will not let my foot slip for He who watches over me will not slumber nor sleep. He who watches over Israel will neither slumber or sleep. The Lord watches over you, the Lord is your shade at your right hand. The sun will not smite you by day nor the moon by night. The Lord will keep you from all harm, He will watch over your life. He will watch over your coming in and your going out forever. The Lord will protect you and preserve your life and He will bless your land. Isa.25:4, You have a shelter for the poor, a refuge for the needy in distress and a shelter from the storm and a shade from the heat. Ps.91:9-11, If you make the most high your dwelling place even the Lord who is my refuge, there will no harm befall you. No disaster will come near your tent, your house where you live in. For He will command His angels concerning you to guard you in all your ways.

For Him to protect you like He said He would, you have to give Him first place in your heart and life. You have to make the most high your dwelling place. You can't do as you please and expect God to keep you from all harm and always protect you everywhere you go and everything you do. You have to do it His way and do His will then He will do what He said He would do for He never lies. He will do His part but you have a part to do also. You can see in many scriptures in the Word of God that there are commands of God in what we have to do to stay in Him and be His child to the end.

Ps. 91:1-6, He who dwell in the shadow of the most high will dwell, or live and will rest in the shadow of the Almighty. You see here, we have to dwell in Him, We have to live in Him to be able to receive all of these promises that He has promised His children. He is my refuge and my fortress, my God in whom I trust. You have to trust Him and He has to be your God. He will save you from the fowler's snare, your enemies, and from the deadly pestilence. He will cover you with His feathers for in His arms and under His wings you will find refuge. His faithfulness will be your shield and rampart, for it's your buckler. Your buckler is your safety. Jesus Christ is your safe keeping. You don't have to fear the terror by night or the arrows, or dangers, by day. You don't have to fear the pestilence or the plagues.

Now, anyone who lives in the real world knows from an experience that belonging to the Lord is not an insurance policy against trials and tribulations or even death. Jesus has promised us that if we serve and follow Him that we were going to have trials and tribulations as long as we live. He also said, it's appointed unto man to die once and then the judgment. God doesn't always rescue you from mortal snares, because lots of them we bring them on ourselves. Sin causes a lot of problems, heartaches and sorrows. The believer who places their trust in God to keep their soul secure will never be disappointed.

When we trust God completely we are eternally secure because God's great love and mercy triumph over evil, He will keep us safe. Our bodies will face challenges and problems but our spirit is kept safe in Jesus Christ our Savior. Our soul can rest securely through Jesus. All make mistakes but we have one who stands in the gap for us and His name is Jesus. He intercedes to God for His children. We cannot continue to sin willfully.

Evil Doers

Ps.125:1, But to those who turn from God to crooked ways, the Lord will banish from them. Sin separates you from God. God does not look upon sin. Isaiah tells us that, no one who walks in the crooked ways will know peace. Isa.59:2, Your iniquities have separated you from God and His face is hidden from you so that He will not even hear you. Verse 9, Justice is for them and righteousness does not reach them. He is saying that there is no righteousness in the sinner person. There is no peace says the Lord for the wicked. Ps.101:4, I will have nothing to do with evil. Prov.24:20, The evil person has no hope for the future. Prov.10:23, A fool finds pleasure in evil conduct. Woe, or sorrow to those that call good evil or call evil good. Children of God are to avoid every kind of evil. John 3:20, Everyone who does evil hates the light. Jesus Christ is the light and in Him there is no darkness, or evil. Jesus said, I am the light of the world and they that follow Me shall not walk in darkness but have the light of life.

The Way out of darkness

Rom.13:12, The night is far spent and the day is at hand, let us therefore cast off the works of darkness and let us put on the armor of light. The Lord is my light and my salvation whom shall I fear or be afraid? For the Lord God is a sun and shield. The Lord will give grace and glory. No good thing will He withhold from them that walk uprightly. Ps.119, Blessed are the undefiled in the way, which walk in the law of the Lord. Blessed are they that keep His testimonies and they that seek Him with their whole heart. With my whole heart have I sought Thee, O let me not wander from Their commandments. Thy Word have I hid in my heart that I may not sin against You. I will meditate in Thy precepts and have respect unto Your ways. I will delight myself in Your statues and I will not forget Your Word. I have declared my ways and You have heard me, teach me Your statues and laws. I have chosen the way to the truth. Teach me O Lord the way of their statues and I shall keep it unto the end.

Now you have seen the Word of God that whosoever abide in Him He will keep you. Mark 13; 13, They that endure to the end the same shall be saved. You must endure in Him to the end. If you start this walk with Jesus and then pull away and walk the other way you will be lost. This is

God's Word not mine. Rev.3; 11, Behold I come quickly, hold fast which you have that no one can steal your crown. Don't let sin and darkness steal your insurance for eternal life. Your salvation is the insurance that will save you in the end. Jesus Christ paid the price when He died on the cross at Calvary. He laid down His life for you and me out of love. Salvation is a gift of God, we didn't earn it or neither can we buy it. Remember, God will not walk away from you but you can walk away from Him. It's each person's choice whom you will serve. Again I will tell you to do what Joshua said, he said to choose this day whom you will serve, but for me and my house we will serve the Lord. Serve Him and let Him take care of you forever.

Cry out for Your Children's Lives

Lam.2:19, Arise, cry out in the night as the watches of the night begins. Pour out your hearts like water in the presence of the Lord, lift up your hands to Him for the lives of your children. We are to have the love for our children that God has for His children. We are to protect them and meet their needs and train them up and nourish them in the Words of the Lord. Deut.6:6-7, Teach your children the commandments of God, talk to them at all times, and impress on them what is right. Train up your children in the right way when they are young and when they're old they will not depart from it. They will never forget what you have told them. We are to correct our children when they are young while there is hope. Do whatever it takes to save their soul from hell, we can't save them but we are to show them the way to the Lord and to do what's right in His sight. We are to seek the Lord and His strength and seek His face continually. He is our strength, our hope and our teacher. He teaches us parents so we can teacher our children.

There are so many children that are not in church today. They are not being taught about God in their homes and they know nothing about God and His goodness. I thank God that I was brought up in a home that loved the Lord and they took me to Church every Sunday and in the week. I thank God that I told my children about Jesus at home. What is going to happen in the next generation if Christ tarries? I beg of you parents to go to church and get saved and teach your children about Jesus Christ so you and your children can be saved from hell and damnation that's coming to all who aren't serving Jesus Christ. There is so much evil in this world today and the children are being caught up in it. Many of them don't even know what's going on. They learn from the evil ones how to curse, steal, kill, hate their parents and many other evil ways of the devil. Parents, you are going to be held accountable to God, for not teaching your children in the right way. You have been given instructions from the Word of God how to raise them and how to train and teach them while they're young before they get out into the evil world.

How long do you spend in prayer for your children? How much fasting do we do? How important is it to get our children into the fold and family of God? We're told to cry out if it takes all night and day. Whatever it takes to see them saved we should do. I Tim.2:8, I therefore that men would pray everywhere, lifting up holy hands without doubt and wrath. Lam.3; 41, Let us lift up our hearts with our hands unto God in Heaven. Gen. 17:18, Abraham prayed for his son Ishmael that he might live for God. II Sam.12:16, David prayed for his son who was sick unto death. He prayed all night with his face to the ground. Job 1; 5, Job prayed for his children continually because he thought they were sinning against God. Matt.17; 15, The father prayer for his demonic child for Jesus to heal him. John 1:41, Andrew lead his brother to Jesus.

Believe for your household to be saved

Acts 16; 31, Paul and Silas said, believe on the Lord Jesus Christ and you and your household shall be saved, your whole family. Acts 2:39, For this promise is for you and unto your children and to all that are afar off even as many as the Lord our God shall call. Who shall tell you words where you and all your house shall be saved? Paul said, as I began to speak the Holy Ghost fell on them as on us in the beginning. They were saved and filled with the Holy Ghost just as they were in the upper room. Jesus is the only one that can save. He said if you will believe with your heart and confess with your mouth that Jesus is Lord and that He died and rose again then you shall be saved. Paul brought them into his house and fed them and rejoiced believing God for all of his house. We have to do the same. We have to stand in the gap for our children and believe God's Word when He said, you and your household shall be saved. Don't ever give up on them. Cry out for them and hold not your peace. He's saying. Tell your children and everyone everywhere about the gospel of the truth. Do not be afraid of what they will say or do to you. Speak and tell them the truth, correct them when needed, stand in the gap for them and do whatever it takes to see them saved. Don't be silent or ignore them. Tell them and plead with them, urge them and be consistent. Don't give up. Jesus said, go preach saying, the Kingdom of God is at hand. I will tell you what to say. For it is not you that speak but the Holy Spirit which speaks through you.

Don't get discouraged

Matt.13; 57, Jesus said, A prophet is without honor in their own town and in their own house. Jesus didn't do many miracles in His own town because of their unbelief. Jesus was a carpenter and grew up there and His family was there and they wondered how He could do all of these things. People, especially family can be very judgmental of their own family. They ask questions like, who are you? What makes you think you can teach or do the work of the Lord? You may have done something when you were young and before you came to know the Lord and they still hold that over your head. But if God has called you to do a work then you need to be obedient and faithful to Him no matter what anyone else says or does. All Christians has a work to do. All are evangelist for Jesus that are saved. You have a story to tell and a testimony of how you come to know the Lord and were born again. He said to tell it wherever you go. It's every Christian's duty to witness to everyone especially to our household.

Remember, we were once in the same place they're in for we were unsaved, lost and on the way to a devil's hell until someone told us about Jesus and the truth in God's Word. I'm sure it took a lot of patience with many of us. Many prayed nights and days for the lost and still are They encouraged us and show us the way and the light until we accepted Jesus Christ in our lives. Don't ever condemn anyone or make then feel they are no good and never will be. Let them know Jesus loves them and wants to save them. Pray that God will do for them what He has done for you. Love them to Christ. For love is the greatest gift of all. Once they are saved, don't leave them but encourage and mentor them in the Lord. Let them know you will always be there for them and so will God.

Children returning home

Isa.59:21, The Lord says, As for Me this is My covenant with them. He's talking about the seed of righteousness. My Spirit that is upon you and My Words which I have put in your mouth shall not depart out of your mouth or out of your seed nor out of your seed's seed, your children or your grandchildren, says the Lord, from hence forth and forever. God has made all of these promises to all generations to all who will believe and accept them and walk in them. Their soul shall dwell at ease and His children shall inherit the earth. God will show His children His covenant. Ps.25; 14, The secret things belong to the Lord and to them that fear Him and He will show them His covenant. These promises are for all of God's children and as many as He shall call. Jesus said. I love them that Love Me and those that seek Me early shall find Me. These are the children that come to Him at an early age. There are lambs in the flock of God. Isa.40; 11, He shall feed His flock like a shepherd. He shall gather the lambs, the little children, with His arms and carry them in His bosom and shall gently lead those that are with young, When my girls were just babies I gave them to the Lord and I never took them back so I believe that they still belong to Him. I believe that they will all come back into the fold for they were all saved at one time. They never lost their belief in Jesus Christ but when they were grown they went their own way. I believe according to the Word of God and by faith that they are coming back home to God.

John 6:45, It is written in the prophets and they shall be taught of God. Everyone therefore that has heard and learned of the Father, comes unto Me. The Bible says that every knee shall bear and every tongue shall confess that Jesus Christ is Lord. It's better to believe and confess now than to wait until the end and then see what you were taught is true but you didn't accept it and then have to confess and be thrown into the lake of fire with the devil and his angels. Ps.71:17, David said, O God, You have taught me from my youth, then and to now. I have declared Thy wondrous works. I am so glad that I can say that the Lord has taught me from my youth and is still teaching me. We never get too old to learn or know too much that we can't be taught more. I am happy also, that I have been able to tell of His wondrous works to others. He has done so much for me and my family. I just want to tell everyone and be in His will always and I am waiting for His returning.

I believe that our children are coming back to the Lord for they were all taught the right way and they all gave their lives to the Lord when they were young. They were even in a ministry of music and have lead others to Christ through their singing. I can see where the Lord has kept His hands on them through the years even though they have not been serving Him with their whole heart. They have never lost their belief in Him. They have gone their way for a season but I believe they are coming back to Christ. Jesus said it and I believe it. We have never stopped praying for them or telling them about their soul. If you have lost children continue to pray for them and never give up on them. Look for them to return to their spiritual home with Jesus. Believe and your whole household shall be saved. There's nothing impossible with God. When it seems like they have gone too far to come back just keep praying for them and claiming God's Word for their salvation. God has made a covenant with His children and He will do all that He said He would do. We have to stand on His Word and believe what He said He will do.

Chapter 12

Your House Can and Will Stand Strong in Battles

Ezek.13:5, You have gone up to the breaks in the wall to repair it for the house of Israel so that it will stand firm in the battle on the day of the Lord. God has made us and our body which is the temple of the Lord. He has saved us and prepared us for whatever we have to go through. We have to live our life to please, honor and obey Him for our house to be able to stand. If we don't let God fix any repairs in our temple, our minds, lust, weaknesses, unbelief or anything that's not lining up with God's will and His ways we are a reproach to others, especially God's people and to Him. Living our lives for God is evidence that our trust is in Him and that we are keeping His commandments. Verses 10-12, Ezekiel said, when there is no peace and there is a broken or weak wall they cover it with white wash. Therefore say to them who cover it with white wash that it's going to fall. Rain will come in, great hail storms and violet winds will burst forth. When the walls fall, people will say to you, where is the white wash that you corrected it with?

When Christian sin or have things in their life that's not of God and they try to cover it up and pretend that everything's alright, it's like white washes, but it won't hold up with God. We can't just repair with anything and expect it to hold up or stand. When our walls are falling down and we get weak the only way to repair it is with Jesus Christ. He is the answer for He is our strength. These Israelites neglected their duties to repair the walls correctly. People are watching how we as Christians are preparing for battles and how we respond in troubles, but most of all God is watching. God longs for us to keep our house, our temple, our body strong in him. He will keep His hedge of protection upon us as long as we stay in His safety zone. Job 1; 10, Has thou not made a hedge about him, above his house and about all that he has on every side? I will take away My hedge or protection and it will be destroyed. If we walk out of God's hedge of protection then we will fall. If we keep His commandments and be obedient to Him then we are in His protection. If we stay in Jesus then we will stand strong in our battles. He is our strength.

Wise and foolish builders

Matt.7:24-27, Therefore everyone who hears these Words of Mine and puts them into practice or does them, is like a wise man that built his house on the rock. The rains came down, the floods rose and the winds blew and beat against that house and it fell not because it was built upon the rock. But everyone who hears these Words of Mine and does not put them into practice or does them, is like a foolish man that built his house upon the sand. The rains came down, the floods came and the winds blew against that house and great was the fall. We have to build on Jesus Christ to stand strong. He's the only way for He is the Rock, the solid Rock for all other ground is sinking sand.

Six things that will make our temple strong for battle

(1) <u>Restraints,</u> Divine restraints, we have to forgive others who do us wrong and we have to ask God to forgive us of our sins. Luke 11:4, And forgive us our sins as we also forgive others who sin against us and lead us not into temptation but deliver us from evil. We have to pray that God will lead us in the right way and keep us from all evil. We have to be careful what we say. Ps.141:3-4, Set a watch O Lord before my mouth, I will keep the door of my lips. Out tongue is like a fire and James said, that we can tame all else but not our tongue. It's a little part of out body but it's can't be tamed. That's why we have to pray and ask God to set a watch over our tongue. Turn not my heart to any evil ways or practice evil works with anyone or let me eat of their dainties, foods. We cannot practice works of the devil or eat food that is made sacrifices to idols. Don't let any evil ways rule over you. Let the words of our mouth and the meditation of our heart be pleasing unto you O Lord, my strength and my Redeemer.

(2)<u>Strength,</u> morally and spiritual, II Sam.22:40, For Thou has girded me with strength to battle those who rose up against me has subsided. They're under me for I have won over them. They that wait upon the Lord shall renew their strength. They shall mount up with wings like an eagle, they shall run and not be weary, and they shall walk and not faint. God said, Fear not for I am with you, I am your God, I will strengthen you, I will help you, I will uphold you with the right hand of My righteousness. Sometimes we just need to be quiet and wait upon the Lord or God.

(3) <u>Beliefs,</u> in divine delays and tests, John 11:4, When Jesus heard that He said, This sickness is not unto death but for the glory of God that the Son of God might be glorified thereby. Sometimes it looks like death when someone is so sick but God allows this so He can do a miracle to show others what He can do so Jesus can be glorified. We should never look at the situation but to the One who can solve the situation, Jesus Christ. I John 3:3, And every one that has this hope or belief, in him purifies himself even as He is pure. Jesus said if you can believe, all things are possible to him that believes. There's nothing that God can't do. First of all else you have to be born again and washed in the blood of Jesus Christ. You have to believe in Jesus Christ and that He was born, walked on this earth, died and was raised again and is coming back for His children, His bride, which is the church. All that believe on Jesus Christ and walk in His ways is His bride.

(4), <u>Security,</u> in the end and it will take your rest in safety. You will lie down with no one to make you afraid and many will count you favor, they will exalt you. You won't have to be afraid for the terror by night or the arrow by day. You shall not be afraid of evil things, your heart is fixed for you are trusting in the Lord. Those who trust in the Lord are like Mt. Zion which cannot be shaken but endure forever. Whoever listens to Me will live in safety and be at ease, without fear of harm. When you lie down you will not be afraid, you shall lie down and your sleep will be sweet. Heb.13:6, So we may boldly say, the Lord is my helper and I will not fear what anyone can do unto me. Love cast out all fear for God is love. As long as you abide in the Lord you have this security.

(5), <u>Daily duties</u> of every believing saints. We are to work and not be idle. Idleness is the work of the devil. Ex.16:4, Then the Lord said unto Moses. I will rain down manna from Heaven for you. The people are to go out and gather each day and gather enough for that day. In this I will test them and see whether they will follow My instructions. God could have rained enough manna for each day but He wanted to see if the people would work for what they were to eat. God wants us to work for our food and for our needs. He doesn't want us to be lazy. He supplies the means and the way but we have to work and walk in His ways. He didn't call anyone just to sit and do nothing.

We are to read His Word. Neh.8:18, Everyday Ezra read from the Book of the law. It's the Bible now but then it was a Scroll. They assembled on the 8th. day to worship. We are to perform our vows to God. We made a vow to Him when we accepted Jesus in our heart and life. That vow was to follow Him all the days of our life. We are to keep that vow and forever perform it. We are to pray and fast. Ps.88:9, David said, I have called upon You daily and I have stretched forth my hands unto You. God wants His children to praise and worship Him through all of the trials and tribulations that we go through. We are to raise our hands to Him for He is worthy of our praise. He works through the praises of His people. He wants us to be watchful. Ps.8:34, Blessed is the one that hear Me, watching daily at My gates waiting at the posts of My door. We have to hear Him and do what He says, not to do our will and way but His. We have to watch and look for Him and we will find Him. We can even feel His presence. We must wait on Him for He will renew our strength daily. He will lead us in the way we should go. Don't walk ahead of Him or behind Him we must walk right along beside Him. Remember, He's never too late for He's right on time. We have to bear our cross .Luke 9:23, He said unto them all, if anyone will come after me let them deny themselves and take up their cross daily and follow Me. We will go through many things in this life that won't be easy but we can't quit or give up. God said, that He would bear our burdens and make them lighter for us if we would bring them to Him. We grow through our trials. We are to encourage one another every day. The strong are to help the weak. We are to stand in the gap for each other.

(6), Endure, We are to hold on to the truth and in our faith. Prov.4:13, Hold on to instructions, do not let go, guard it well for it is your life. They that endure to the end the same shall be saved. Blessed are the ones that endure temptation for when they are tried they shall receive the crown of life which the Lord has promised them that love Him. James 5; 11, Behold we count them happy which endures. You have heard of the patience of

Job and have seen his end. We saw what the Lord brought about in job's life. God is full of compassion, love and mercy. Job said, the righteous shall hold on to his ways and he who has clean hands shall be stronger and stronger. We should never grow weary in well doing for we will reap if we faint not. Jesus said to continue in your love for Him. Continue to abide in Him. We are to continue in what we have learned from the Holy Scriptures because it will make us wise for salvation through faith in Jesus Christ. Heb.12:1, Lay aside every weight that so easily besets you or hinders you from serving the Lord and run the race with patience that is set before you. Don't let sin enter into your mind, body or deeds. Cast off every evil imagination and spirit. Rev.3:11, and 16:15, Behold I come quickly, hold fast which you have that no one take your crown. Behold I come as a thief in the night. Blessed are they that are watching for Me and keep their garments clean.

Our Spiritual garments consist of these. You will find them in Epe.6:14-18. The belt of truth, breastplate of righteousness, our feet shod with the preparation of the gospel, shield of faith, helmet of salvation, sword of the Spirit, the Bible, and prayer in the Spirit. If we do these we will endure to the end. We can stand strong only when we abide in the Lord. Die to self daily and let Him live through and in you. We have to stand firm and stay true to Jesus Christ to endure to the end.

God said He would fight our battles

Jer.21:5, I God, will fight your battles. He said, I will fight against your enemies with an out stretched hand and a mighty arm in anger and fury and great wrath. He said, do not be afraid or discouraged because of the vast army, for the battle is not yours but Mine. Don't be afraid of all of your big problems or troubles for I will take care of them. We have a big God, He's bigger than any problem we could ever have. He said to take your position and stand strong and see the deliverance of the Lord. Go on and face your problems for the Lord will be with you. Have faith in the Lord your God for He will uphold you. You can begin to give thanks unto the Lord even before you see the problem disappear. Give God the thanks and glory before He even meets your needs. God works through the praises of His people. Start singing praises unto God and see what He does. We are to be strong and courageous and not afraid or discouraged. Greater is He that is within us than he that is in the world. The enemy is only the arm of flesh but God is all power.

Little David said to the Philistine, the giant, you come against me with a sword and a javelin but I come against you in the name of the Lord Almighty, the God of armies of Israel whom you have defiled. All He needed was the name of God to win his battle. You know the story. He killed the giant with a little stone, all in the name of God. What kind of battle are you going through? There is no battle to big for God to take care of. Just give it to Him, trust Him and wait with patience and He will work it out.

Four things we need to do when we face a problem or battle

(1), Identify the problem.

(2), Present it to Jesus

(3), Do what He says

(4), Rest in the peace of God.

We are to keep on with our work, stay alert but keep working. Prayer, and alert actions go hand in hand for we are to watch and pray. Be obedient to God's Word always. Even in the midst of conflicts and struggles, allow your heart to rest and find shelter and peace in God's leadership. The battles may surround you but here's peace in the promises of God. God said, My presence will go with you and I will give you rest. Ex.14; 14, The Lord will fight for you and you will hold your peace. We can win the battles of evil influence of others. We have power over our enemy. God is our power. We have enemies in high places but we don't have to worry about them for God will take care of them. Epe.6; 12, For we wrestle not against flesh and blood but against principalities, powers and the rulers of darkness of this world and against spiritual wickedness in high places. The devil is everywhere but we have the power over him in the name of Jesus. Peter said to be sober, be vigilant because your adversary, the devil walks around as a roaring lion, seeking whom he may devour. He can only do what you allow him to do.

God sees everything

II Chr.16:9, For the eyes of the Lord run to and fro through out the whole earth to show Himself strong in the behalf of them whose heart is perfect toward Him. The angels encamps around about them that fear Him and He delivers them. God said He would cover you with His feathers and under His wings shall you trust, for His truth shall be your shield and your buckler. You are protected by God if you are one of His children. Ps.125:2, As the mountains are around Jerusalem so the Lord is around His people from now and forever more.

God is our divine protestor. Luke 21:18, There shall not a hair of your head perish. There is complete protection from our God for His people. With God we have the victory and He will trample down our enemies. Our enemies can be those of our household or even ourselves. He said He would take care of all our problems if we would give them to Him. We need to leave them there with Him and trust him and wait with patience. Don't pick them back up again and try to carry them. So many times we carry things to God but then we worry about them and pick the burdens back up again. God doesn't need our help or direction on how to fight our battles. He knows just what we need and what to do with every situation. He knows what we are going to go through even before the problem starts. He already had a plan to fix the problem before we knew about the problem. If we would just learn to trust Him in all things and let Him do what is right for us there would be less worry and fretting. Worry is sin for when you worry then you are not trusting God with all of your heart. Remember, God sees and knows all things and has the answer for everything small or great. Let Him fight your battles and you will win.

Chapter 13

Life Is Tough But God Is Faithful

Gal.6:9, Let us not grow weary in well doing for we will reap if we faint not. Don't ever give up or give in to your problems, for with God you are a winner. Don't worry about the things that you can't change but change the things that you can and leave the rest to God. Don't fret and complain for that is doubt. Just trust God first of all and then yourself knowing that you can do all things through the Lord Jesus Christ. You and God are a majority and you are a winner with Him.

Three things we can see in this scripture. (1), We will reap if we don't faint. (2), Don't quit when things gets bad. (3) Don't quit on God or yourself and others. For with God we will gain the victory. For whosoever is born of God overcomes the world and this is the victory that overcomes the world, even our faith. The just shall live by faith. The just are those who have been born again, washed in the blood of Jesus and are following Him with their whole heart and life. Without faith we cannot please God. So if God said it you have to believe it and never doubt. For the person who doubts will receive nothing. Remember what David says in Ps.46:1, He is our very present help in time of troubles. He will never leave or forsake His children and that's His promise to us. Always stand on His Word and claim the victory no matter what you are going through in this life. There's nothing too big for God to handle and nothing too small that He doesn't care about.

Prov.3:5-6, Trust in the Lord with all of your heart and lean not upon your own understanding. In all your ways acknowledge Him and He will direct your paths. Some say that Christians should never ask God any questions. But I believe that God wants us to have such a relationship with Him that we can be ourselves. He knows what we are thinking anyway so why not confront Him with it. We should never question His ability or decisions or His answers for He always knows what's best for each one of His children. You need to tell Him, Lord I love You and I trust You and I rest in the fact that you know how I feel but I put it all into Your hands. He wants us to have a genuine relationship with Him and not just something half-hearted. He wants us to tell Him that we trust Him and is in control of our lives and that we know that He never makes a mistake. Tell Him that you stand on His Word and that you know He's going to take care of you. Pray to God that He will help you glorify Him through all that you are going through. God works through the praises of His people.

Hosea 6:3, As surely as the sun rises, He will appear, bringing refreshments and renewal. Praise God. When we feel hopeless and empty we can be encouraged in the fact that God's a God of great reversal. He is always there with us to help us because He is always faithful to His Word and to His children. We don't have to understand what is going on but we need to trust Him and lean not on our own understanding. We know that God can turn our despair and sorrows into jubilations, joy. For the joy of the Lord is our strength. God knows we are human and we have our weak moments and He understands where we are and what we are going through. He is our strength and in His strength we have the joy of the Lord. Don't be weary in well doings.

When my husband, Leon was so ill in 2002, I relied on this scripture in Proverbs. I thought I had to understand what was going on and why Leon was so ill. But God told me that I didn't need to understand but lean on Him and trust Him with all of my heart and He would see us through. I believed it and stood on those Words of God. I even kept myself away from doubting people and from all negative conversations. Even when the doctors would give me a bad report I would just say, you're telling us what you know medically but I know what my God says and I will stand on it. I never doubted that Leon wasn't going to get well because God had given me complete peace. There were many Christians that prayed with me and then would turn right around and say, he's just not going to make it. They were looking at what they saw, because he did look like death itself. You can't believe what you always see for that's not faith. I kept myself in the

Word of God day and night to retain my faith in the bad times. In all your ways acknowledge Him and He will direst your paths. Believe!!

God made a covenant to His children

This covenant God made, He will always remember it forever. He raised up a Horn of salvation for us, Jesus Christ, His only begotten Son. Luke1:68-75, He prophesied through His holy prophets long ago. We have salvation from our enemies and from the hand of all who hate God's children. His covenant is to show mercy to the fathers of old and to remember His covenant. The covenant He swore to Abraham still stands today. For God never changes, He's the same yesterday, today and forever. The covenant is to rescue His children from the hand of their enemies and enable us to serve Him without fear. He does make a way for His children, those that follow Him and are obedient to Him. The covenant is for all who will live in holiness and righteousness all of your days. God said, we can worship Him without fear. This is God's Word and we can stand on it, always. We don't have to worry and fret about what is going on in this world as long as we are His children. Worry and trust don't go together, worry is sin because you are not leaning and trusting totally on God.

What have you committed to God?

II Tim.1:12, God said, He would keep what we have committed to Him from that day. What have you committed to Him? Have you given Him your all? Have you given Him your children, family and friends? If you have given Him much then He will keep you from much. He wants all of you not just part of you. Some Christians hold on to some things in their life that they need to give up. Some of these things might not keep you out of Heaven but will cause you to loose blessing here on this earth. Some things will even shorten your days on earth and cause you to have a lot of sickness and bad health. Ask yourself this question, is it worth holding on to? Have you committed your time to Him? Have you committed your money to Him? Have you committed your whole life to Him? That's what God wants, all of you and everything. You know. It all belongs to Him anyway. If He didn't give you good health then you couldn't work to make the money for the things you have. He's the giver of life, strength and your entire being. If you think that you have something that you just can't seem to give up, just try Jesus. He will replace what you think is so important for other things that will fulfill your life in such a way that you will wonder, what took so long for me to commit it to the Lord. Your desires and your want to will change completely. Being totally committed to God is the best life you can ever live here on this earth. The blessings of God and your relationship with Him will be so fulfilling. Your cup will be over full in Jesus Christ. Ps.125:1, Those that trust in the Lord are like Mt. Zion which cannot be shaken but endure forever. The Lord will protect and preserve their lives, they will be blessed in the land, all that serve Him. David said, he had never seen the righteous forsaken nor his son begging for bread. Don't let what's going on in this world today keep you in turmoil and fear, but trust in the Word of the Lord with all of your heart ,soul, mind and your strength, Draw near to God and He will draw near to you. God has not given you a spirit of fear but a sound mind. Look up for your Redemption draws near. Jesus is coming soon.

God is bringing judgment on America

America has been the land of the free, home of the brave, land of blessing and a place where we can worship God and feel free and not be in danger. We have had freedom of worship in America. God has so blessed our nation but people are living more evil than ever before. Our young people and children are not being told about Jesus Christ as they were when we were growing up. The morals have changed the dress codes, the filthy language and crime. I can't believe what comes out of some of our young people. The older generation has fallen away from the principals of God. America is in great danger for denying our Lord, Jesus Christ. In fact, all nations are in great danger of judgment from God. But America was a Christian nation. This nation was founded on Christianity. People have used their freedom to do the things they want to do and not to please and worship God. Many in other nations are losing their lives because they believe and worship God, our Heavenly Father. We have been so blessed in America. The question is, how much longer will America be blessed? I believe that the many storms, earthquakes, tornados and all of the disasters that are going on are judgments from God for sin and disobedience to God. Just as Moses stood in the gap for Israel, I believe that all Christians should stand in the gap for America and all of the other nations as well. Israel was in bondage and people hated them and many nations still hate them today because they're God's chosen people. Thank God, America still stand for Israel and still support them. Come to Jesus and live.

The Lord will stand by you

Acts 23:11, And the Lord stood by Paul and said, be of good cheer for as you have testified of Me in Jerusalem so must you bear witness also in Rome. Paul in all his problems of being in jail, beaten and mocked, didn't ask any questions when the Lord told him that He was standing by and was with him. We need to listen and not ask any questions or worry about things, Paul said nothing. He just listened to the Lord for he trusted God and we need to trust Him in all things as well.

God send ministering angels to help us

Acts 27:23-25, For there in the night stood an angel of God. The angels are God's servants. We all have assigned angels from God to help us. This angel was encouraging Paul in the storm of the sea. Fear not Paul, the angel said unto him, be of good cheer for I believe God, that it shall be as it was told me. We need to believe what God says and accept His report. Paul and all the men landed safe on shore even though the ship was broken in pieces. God will and does deliver His children safe and secure. We are in His hands if we stay grounded in Him and do His will. Just as the Lord stands by you and me and is true to us we are to stand true to Him also. When God ask His children to do something we should do it. Mark 3:5, When Jesus told the man with the withered hand to stretch it forth to Him the man did and the Lord healed his hand. So many time Christians lose their blessings because they don't obey God. Jesus Christ is standing waiting to do something for His children but you have to do something first. You have to ask and believe that what you ask for is going to come to pass. Mark 9:23, If you believe all things are possible to them that believe. Matt.9:29, According to your faith be it unto you. How much faith do you have?

Isaiah says, The Lord said, fear not I will help you. I am with you so don't be dismayed or disappointed for I am your God. I will strengthen you and I will help you. I will hold you with the right hand of My righteousness. I have redeemed you and have called you by your name, you are Mine. When you pass through the waters I will be with you, when you go through the rivers they shall not over flow you. When you walk through the fire you shall not be burned neither shall the flames be upon you. For I am the Lord your God the Holy One of Israel.

We are to rejoice through our problems

Prov.17:22, A merry heart does good like a medicine but a broken spirit dries the bone. Jesus said, In Me you will have peace. Be of good cheer for I have overcome the world. Hold on to God and trust Him in everything for He is in control and He will stand by you. He will never leave or forsake you, this He has promised this and all who will follow Him and be obedient to Him. Paul said, rejoice in the Lord always and again I say rejoice. Even though we may be sorrowful we can still have joy in our hearts. We may not be happy in all things but we can always have joy because we know in whom we believe, Jesus Christ. We know that He is able to keep what we have committed to Him against that day. What day? That day when we are having problem so big that we don't feel we can go on. And also, the days of the great tribulation that's coming to the whole world, for all who reject Him as Lord and Savior. He will keep all believers from those terrible days. Are you one of His? If not, accept Him today and stand with Him and He will stand with you, always.

God is the way for He is our provider

Through the difficulties of this life's journey God will make a way for His children. He did it for the Israelites and he will still do it for His children today. There is only one true God and there is none other. The Lord Almighty is His name. As long as you will be faithful and obedient to Him, He will make a way and provide for you.

Ex.14:16, God departed the water and the Israelites crossed over on dry land. They were saved from the Egyptians killing them. We can't just live any ole way but we have to live holy and righteous in the Lord our God. Our righteousness is as filthy rags so we have to live in His righteousness.

If you live your way then you can't live in His righteousness. He said He would make the way straight for the righteous. No one is perfect but we are to strive to be perfect just as He is perfect. He said that He would go before you and make the crooked places straight. Isa.40:4, Every valley shall be exalted or lifted up and every mountain or hill shall be made low and the crooked places made straight and the rough places plain. What God is saying here is this. There is no valley too low that He can't reach down and take care of us. There is no mountain or hill too tall that He can't reach us. There is nothing too bent or out of shape that He can't make straight again. He promised to go before us and make the way for His children.

Jesus said, just believe

Matt.21:21, Jesus said unto them, if you have faith as a mustard seed you can say to this mountain, be removed and cast into the sea and it will have to move. By faith you can remove obstacles out of the way, in Jesus name. We can't do it on our own power but in the power in Jesus Name. Jesus does it through us, His children. As you will notice, I keep saying, His children. All of His promises are for those who have been born again and who are following Him and doing His will. These are His children. His promises are not for the world and the sinners. The only promise for the lost is where they are going for rejecting Jesus Christ as your Savior. There are promises of God for you after you get saved. Believe what you ask and it shall be done unto you. To get to Heaven you must believe. Do you believe that God is your provider? Then you must trust and lean on Him. Do you believe that God is your helper? Then you have to let Him do it His way and not yours. His way is not always your way. He is the truth, the way and the life and no one comes to Father but through Jesus Christ. He is the way maker. Jesus has made a way to our eternal home and all we have to do is follow Him. Praise the Lord.

There is Joy in the Presence of the Lord

God created us to have fellowship with Him. When we talk with Him it makes Him happy and makes us content. There is joy in the presence of the Lord. We can totally rest in the presence of the Lord. We can totally rejoice in His promises. God's Word is eternal. His laws and commandments has

129

always endured and always will, they are righteous and trust worthy. We know that God's love is unfailing. God is always good in all that He does. The joy of our heart comes from understanding and following the ways of the Lord, Heb.12:1, If we want to be completely happy we must throw off everything that hinders us and the sin that so easily besets us. We can have joy in our hearts and soul even when everything around us is going wrong. Ps.91:1, They who dwell in the shelter of the most high will rest in the shadow of the Almighty. We do have joy in rest. We can sing for joy to God who is our strength. He removes the burdens from our shoulders. If we keep our minds and our hearts constantly on blessings instead of disasters and negatives, our lives will be enriched and happy then we can grow even through the hard times and experiences from calamities we face.

Ps.119:138, We can set our eyes on the future with confidence and a firm hope in God's grace, protection and care because all of God's statues or laws are fully trust worthy. We don't have to worry about what the economy does or what's going to happen in our world today because God is in control and He said that He would never leave or forsake His children. The greatest way to be in God's presence is to praise, worship and seek His presence. David said, When you cling to God and you refuse to let go He is there with you and He upholds you. Then we will have the joy of His presence. He said, I have seen You in the sanctuary and beheld Your glory. To behold His glory is awesome and life changing. When God's glory falls you are completely in His presence. There is nothing like this experience of God. We can't do anything without God's anointing and do it right but when God's glory and power falls we can do nothing because we are completely in His presence and under His power.

Give your all to Him

Ps.37:4-6, Delight yourselves in the Lord and He will give you the desires of your heart. Commit your ways unto Him, trust Him and He will do it. He will make your righteousness shine like the dawn of justice of your cause like the noon day. Trust in the Lord and do good. Dwell in the land and enjoy safe pasture. If our life delights in the Lord then all our desires are fulfilled. When someone else sees the joy in us it usually rubs off. We find what we want is what He wants. He delights in honoring our hearts desires we are in the center of His will. I Pet.8-9, As we believe in Him and grow to love Him more everyday we will be filled with inexpressible and glorious joy, the eternal salvation of our soul. We can enjoy God through our experiences.

As you trust God and the desire for more of Him increases, He will lead you deeper into His glory until you are surrounded by His presence.

Vision of the Holy waters

Ezek. 47:1-5, When Ezekiel's guide brought him to the door of the temple there was water gushing from under the threshold and the water was ankle deep. Then as he went on the water became knee deep. Then it became loin deep, up to the ribs. Finally it became like a river too high to pass over. Ankle deep is where one first steps into the water of life. When one first get saved and accepts Jesus Christ as their Lord and Savior. They are just learning so they are just a little wet, but still saved. Then as they and striving to do what is right in the Lord. As they continue to grow they finally get into the water that's loin or rib deep. They have progressed spiritually in Jesus. It's about now that they are praying and asking God to baptize them with the Holy Ghost. They have been saved and Jesus came into their life but now they desire the power of the Holy Ghost to be in them. So the water is now over their heads. It was so deep that they could swim in it. The Holy Ghost takes over their life. Now it is joy and unspeakable and full of glory. God's river of joy is flowing out of you. He wants to satisfy your soul and needs spiritually and desires to give you complete joy in the Lord. What's holding you back from receiving the baptism of the Holy Ghost? Many have a form of godliness but reject the power thereof. They believe in the Lord Jesus Christ but they deny the power of the Holy Ghost. There is power in the Holy Ghost. We can all grow in the Lord for He is still working on us. We can never learn too much and we will never know it all until we make it into the Kingdom of Heaven and talk with Jesus and be like Him. Of course, once we've made it in and everything is so wonderful then we probably won't even think about what we may think we will ask Jesus then.

Not a smooth sailing but a safe landing

Jesus never promised us a smooth sailing or walk with Him but He does promise us a safe and prosperous landing. We have to go through many things here on this earth but He will be with us to make a way for us. Lot of people has to go through bad sicknesses in order to find Christ. The sailing is not too good but the outcome is great.

Luke 4:35-41, Jesus healed the sick right then instantly not later. The demonic man was healed at once. Jesus said to the demon, come out of him it came out at once. He went to Simon Peter's house and found his mother-in law was sick with fever. Jesus stood over her and rebuked the fever and it left her immediately and she stood up and ministered unto them. As the sun was going down all of them that were sick with diver diseases came to Jesus and He healed all of them immediately. Even devils came out of many and declared that He was Christ the Son of God. Jesus rebuked them and told them not to speak. So you see that even devils believe and confess Jesus Christ as the Son of God. There's another lesson in this and that is, we have to do more than just believe, we must act upon our belief.

Mark 6:45-51, Jesus walked on the water, now. Jesus sent His disciples to get into the ship to go to the other side to Bethel. When they had gone He went into the mountain to pray. He saw them toiling in their rowing of the ship for the winds were beating against them. In the night He came walking on the water. When they saw Him they thought it was a ghost and cried out. They were all troubled and afraid so He said to them, be of good cheer for it is I, be not afraid. He went to them and the winds were calmed right away. They were amazed that the winds obeyed Jesus. If the winds obey why can't you?

Mark 4:35-41, Jesus calmed the storm now. This was another storm in the sea that Jesus calmed down. The disciples were in the boat and were sailing along when a great storm rose and the winds were blowing. The waves were beating against the ship and by now the ship was full of water. They were so afraid. Jesus was asleep in the back of the boat and they awoke Him and said, Master do you care that we perish? Jesus arose and rebuked the winds and the waves and said, peace be still and they stopped immediately. Jesus asked them, why are you so afraid and have so much fear? How is it that you have no faith? They still feared exceedingly and asked among themselves, what kind of man is this that even the winds and the waves obey Him? Jesus said in another scripture, Oh ye of little faith.

I Pet.4:12, Beloved, think it not strange concerning the fiery trials which is to try you as though it was some strange thing that is happening to you. That the trial of your faith being much more than gold that perishes though it be tried with fire might be found unto praise, honor and glory at the appearing of Jesus Christ. Your faith will never perish for it will stand when all else fails. The just shall live by faith and without faith you cannot please God. James 1:22-3, My brethren, count it all joy when you fall into diver temptations. Knowing this, that the trying of your faith works patience.

Acts 15:22, Those who continue in faith must go through many tribulations to enter into the Kingdom of God. We can see here that God doesn't promise His children a smooth sailing. We have to go through some bad times as well as some good times. This is the way He has to test us so we can prove to Him that we mean business with Him. If everything went our way and good all of the time we might feel we didn't need Him. If we didn't have problems how would we know that He would or could solve them? James said that we should rejoice when we are going through trials knowing that He was going to make a way for us. We are not to be happy for the trial but happy because we know that He will bring us out just like He did for the disciples.

Ps.119:71 and 143-144, David said, it was good for me to be afflicted so that I could learn your degrees. We learn to lean more on Jesus through every trial and test we have. Troubles and distress have come upon me but Your commands are my delight. Your statues or laws are forever right, give me understanding that I may live. I called on the Lord in my distress and He heard and answered me. David didn't say that the Lord waited but that He answered him. There are times when the Lord will say wait awhile or He might even say no. There are many times He will answer right away. We have to wait upon the Lord for He knows the right time.

The Lord will keep you from harm. He will watch over your life. He will over your coming in and your going out. So you see, He has promised us a safe landing if we will just endure to the end in Him. None of us know what tomorrow will bring. We don't know about tomorrow but this one thing we do know, we know who holds our hands. He has promised us a place of happiness, peace, good health, wealth, love and a place of rest forever for all who abide in Him. Our safe landing is Heaven with Jesus Christ and all of our loved ones forever. That is worth everything that we may have to go through down here on this earth and in this life. Jesus is coming soon so be ready, watching and waiting for His returning to take us to our new home, our safe landing.

Chapter 14

The Cure is Jesus Christ

*J*er.30:12-13, This is what Jeremiah said to Israel, Your wound is incurable, your injury beyond healing. There is no one to plead your cause. No remedy for your sore, no healing for you. He's talking about the sinners not the church. Lost souls cannot be cured by moral beings, moral living or religious people. No person or nation can heal a lost soul. Only the Lord Jesus Christ can save the lost. It's through Him only that you can be saved and forgiven of your sins.

Jesus is our deliverer, our healer and our Lord and Savior. He's the Savior because He saves and He's the Son of God. At times we as Christians may feel helpless. Maybe your sinful past is making accusations at you and making you feel you're not saved anymore. Maybe you have turned your back on God who sometimes seem slow to answer you. But He is always on time. When you are restless or broken and feel so alone, here's what our Heavenly Father does for you. Ps.147:3, Our Father lovingly waits to bind up our wounds, heals us and forgives us. Our Lord Jesus Christ is the only cure for our spiritual problems of life. When you call upon Him, He hears and answers for He loves you and His mercy endures forever. Don't let the devil or other people put you down. When you feel down cast just look toward Heaven and call on Jesus.

Our future is hopeful in Jesus Christ. Jer.29:11-14, For I know the plans I have for you, declared the Lord. I have plans to prosper you not to harm you, plans to give you hope and a future. You will seek Me and find Me when you seek Me with your whole heart. I will be found by you declares the Lord. These Words and promises are for all of His children today and forever. He does not change and His Word does not change for He's the same forever. God knows your future and He wants you to trust Him all of the way. When we feel abandoned He promised His presence. When we are tired for waiting for our dreams, desires and wants He promised strength to wait. He's trying to teach us patience. No matter how bleak our circumstances look God's promise hope and a future for His children. When you pray in faith and God doesn't show up when you think He will or should, don't get discouraged. He always comes through at the right time.

Our God is a God of reversals

Hosea 6:3, As surely as the sunrises He will appear bringing refreshments and reversals. God can turn anything that looks bad to something that is good. He can turn the sick into good health. He can turn financial problems into wealth and prosperity. There is nothing impossible for God. When you feel empty and hopeless you can be encouraged by the fact that our God is a God of great reversals. He can make good come out of the bad situations. He can turn what seem to be bad into good. He can change any situation in a moment. God can and does turn despair into jubilation. He can and does turn sorrows into joy. Just as the soft rain in spring cleans, brighten and restores so does God come to His people when they truly repent and turn to Him with all of their heart. When Christians sin and then come to God and repent our faithful God is there with forgiveness and restoration with such love and compassion for them. He does not with hold Himself from you when you call on Him.

When you feel yourself sinking fast, do not resign yourself to your problems. Rather, you need to choose to pray to God in humble faith. His salvation is sure and His love is unconditional. Jesus is the cure for everything, physically and spiritually. Our hope is in Him only. People will fail you, your friends and family will fail you but He will never fail you. He said He would never leave or forsake you and that He would go with you until the end.

Hope is a precious gift of salvation

Hosea 6:19, Hope is a precious gift of salvation. We have this hope in Jesus and we are anchored to that Rock for our soul is firm and secure. If we stay in Him and endure to the end, we are secure in Jesus Christ our Lord and Savior. Don't give up just because things don't look good but look to Him. Remember that He is a God of reversals and whatever He does with your situations in this life, you just trust Him for He knows what He's doing and He never makes a mistake. He is all knowing and all loving, He's the beginning and the end. He knows the beginning from the end. God is working in the Spiritual realm to accomplish His perfect will in your life and mine. We all need to wait upon Him and be patient, trust Him and praise Him for the answer. Don't complain, grumble or fret while you wait. Leave it all in His hands for He knows how to work it all out for your good. We need to learn to ask His will be done and not ours. If you worry about anything then you are not trusting Him to do what you asked of Him, or what He feels is best for you now.

Ps.139: 1-6, O Lord, You have searched me and You know me. You know when I sit and when I rise. You understand my thoughts afar off. You discern my going out and my lying down, You are familiar with all my ways. Before a word is on my tongue, You know it completely, Oh Lord. You have hemmed me in behind and before and you have laid your hand upon me. Such knowledge is too wonderful for me. It is high and I can't attain it. God can read our thoughts and our hearts. How often do we think or say, I don't want anyone to know about this or something in my life. You may have spent lots of time and energy at trying to hide your past or something you've done in your life because of the risk of rejection or love from others. Someone knows and that's God. You cannot hide anything from Him for He sees and knows everything. He still loves you in spite of your past and what you may have done. In human relationships love is so conditional many times. But with God it is different. His love is genuine and unconditional to you and me. Verse 13, There is nothing that God doesn't know for He created us in our mother's womb. There's nothing about us that He doesn't know. There is nothing that's on our minds and hearts that He doesn't know before we speak or do it. Nothing catches Him by surprise because He already knows it. Verse 24, Because of His unfailing devotions to us, He is committed to searching our hearts and revealing to us any offensive way so we can walk a straight path toward our eternal home.

You can't hide from God

Ps. 139:7-10, Where can I go from Your Spirit? Where can I flee from Your presence? If I go to Heaven You are there and if I make my bed in hell You are there. If I take the wings of the dawn, or morning or if I settle on the far side of the sea, even there Your hand will guide me, your right hand will hold me fast. David is saying here, there is no where he can ever go that God doesn't see him. It's the same with us today. That should never be a bad thing. I praise Him that He knows where I am and He's with me. I want His hand to always guide me. I want Him to be with me each day that I wake up for I would never want to face a day without Him on my side and being with me. Praise God, He knows where I am at all times. He's my keeper and salvation, He's my strength and the joy of my life. He's a very presence help in time of trouble.

God's thoughts are precious

Verses 17-18, How precious to me are Your thoughts O God, how great are the sum of them. If I would count them they would out number the grains of the sand. When I'm awake I am still with you. We will never know just how much God has done for us. Just to know His thoughts are upon me is too great for me to understand or tell. I look back on my life and I see so many times He's come through for me it's almost over flows my mind and concepts . He's kept me from so many dangers and there are more that I don't even know about. We need to search ourselves to make sure there is no hidden sin that can keep us from being in the will of God. Verses 23-24, David said, search me O God and lead me in the way everlasting. We need to ask God to search our hearts and ways to make sure everything is in order. Our thoughts should be on Him and not on ourselves. It's not about me but about Him who died for me. As His thoughts are on you then your thoughts should always be on Him.

We can know God's will for our lives

John 16:13-15, The Holy Spirit will lead you into all truth. He will make it known to you. All that belong to the Father is Mine that is why I said, The Spirit will make it known to you. It would be much easier for us if we had a roadmap so we could see from one place to the other where we were going, someone said. If we could see the path we think it would be easy, but if we saw all of the curves, potholes and detours it would make us afraid. We have to go through many tribulations if we follow Christ, Paul said. Many times we can't see the light at the end of the tunnel. If we could see the end it would sure help. But we have to go in faith in God knowing that He will bring us through our problems. The Bible is our road map and we need to read it faithfully to find what Jesus wants us to do. He will show us His will for us if we will just follow Him and trust Him with all of our hearts, minds, soul and strength. Without faith you cannot please God. The just shall live by faith in Him. Titus 3:8, Devote yourself to doing what is good for this is profitable for everyone. Sometimes you may feel torn apart and your human flesh cries out for comfort and direction. It in on the path with Christ that you will find rest, comfort and the right direction. Ps.25:9, The meek will He guide in judgment and the meek will He guide in their way. Ps.32:8, I will instruct you and teach you in the way you should go and I will guide you with My own eye.

We need to pray for His will to be done

Ps.143:10, Teach me to do Your will for You are my God. Your Spirit is good. Lead me into the land of righteousness. Too often we fail to ask God what His will is for us and what we're doing. You can get yourself in lots of trouble without consulting God's will for you. Many are in trouble today financially because they never ask God what they should do. There are many marriages in trouble because they didn't seek God for the right spouse. God will never lead His children astray for He has the very best for His them. He wants you and me to live happy on this earth. Jesus prayed to the Father to have His will be done on earth as it is in Heaven. Ps.27; 11, David prayed to God and said, teach me O Lord and lead me in a plain path. He was saying, lead me in a simple ways and not just in the big things of life. Our everyday path should be lead by God. Let Him be in charge all of the time. I Tim.2:8, I want people everywhere to lift up holy hands in prayer without anger or disputing. We need to praise God more, praise Him in everything. I Thessalonians 5:18, Be joyful always, pray continually. Give thanks in all circumstances for this is the will of God for you in Jesus Christ. Sometimes it's hard to praise God when things are going bad and all hell seem to be coming against us but we have been told to pray, be joyful and give thanks always. You don't have to thank God for the problems but thank Him for you know He will make a way for you to get through the problems.

Sometimes He leads in different places and ways

Deut. 8:2, And you shall remember all the way which the Lord thy God led you forty years in the wilderness to humble you and to prove you to know what was in your heart whether you would keep His commandments. God had the Israelites in the wilderness for all of those years to teach them something. He still has us in the wilderness at times to teach us too. The quicker we learn the better we will be. God does test His children but He does not tempt anyone. We grow through the hard times if we stay in in Him and keep His commandments. If everything was good then we wouldn't know that God would do what He said but He knows just what it takes for each one of us to become humble and obedient to Him. Don't get so comfortable in your easy chair and feel you can't be humbled. The Bible says that when you feel you're so strong that you can't fall to watch out. For when you feel this way watch out lest you fall. We stand in God's strength. He is our strength and sometimes we have to be put down to see that it's Him that is strong and it is Him that is carrying us.

God's children hear Him

We are of God and they that know God hears us. God knows His children by name. We know when God is speaking to us and He hears us when we speak to Him. Luke 12:12, For the Holy Spirit shall teach you in the same hour what you ought to say. David said, I delight to do your will O God. We should always seek His will for our lives. Matt. 12:50, For whosoever shall do the will of My Father which is in Heaven, the same is My brother, sister and My mother. We are His family and He loves us.

We obtain knowledge through our acquaintance with God. Hosea 6:3, Then we shall know if we follow on to know the Lord. His going forth is prepared as the morning and He shall come unto us as the rain, as the latter rain and the former rain unto the earth. He will give His children Spiritual knowledge. The latter rain is the filling of the Holy Spirit, the former rain is when we got saved.

Obedience is the condition of receiving

John 7:12-17, Jesus said, My doctrine is not Mine but Him that sent Me. If anyone shall do His will, he shall know of the doctrine whether it is of God or whether I speak of myself. Jesus told the Jews which believed on Him, If you continue in My will then you are My disciple. You can believe and not follow Jesus and you can still be lost. Faith alone is not good enough for you have to have faith with works. The devil believes and trembles. Believe on the Lord and you shall be saved but He goes on to say, follow Me. If you follow Him then you will do His will and receive everlasting life. You have to do something to receive. You have to be obedient and faithful to Jesus Christ. John 8:32, And you shall know the truth and the truth shall set you free. Jesus said, if any person will come after Me let them deny yourself and take up their cross and follow Me. Acts 22; 14 says that you shall know His will. There is no excuse in not knowing what God wants of us. Epe.1:9, Having made known to us the mystery of His will according to the good pleasure which He has purposed in Himself. God has made enough known to His children for all to know His will for them. John 10:4, And when Jesus puts forth His own sheep, He goes before them and the sheep follow Him for they know His voice. Verse 27, My sheep know My voice and I know them and they follow Me.

The rule of everyday

James 4:5, For what we ought to say is, if it's the Lord's will we shall do this or that. The world will pass away but they that do the will of God abide forever. Jesus wants our heart and our eyes to observe His ways. John said, hereby we do know that we know Him if we keep His commandments. If you are not living the life that Jesus has told you to live and you're not keeping the commandments then you don't know Him. You may know about Him but to know Him and to know about Him are two different things. Many people know about Him but they don't have a relationship with Him. To know Him is to love Him, and to love Him is to serve Him. Rom.12:1, Paul said, I beseech you brethren by the mercies of God, that you present your bodies a living sacrifice holy and acceptable unto God which is your reasonable service. We as Christians are to be careful that our life lines up with the Word of God. We are to keep our bodies pure and holy without committing sin. Let everyone that names the name of Christ depart from iniquity. Let no sin reign in your body or life.

We know as we have read and been taught what God's will is for our lives. We are to keep His commandments, keep our bodies holy, deny self, be obedient to Him in all things, be obedient to parents, sin not and love one another, study to show ourselves approved a workman for Him, pray continually, and seek Him always. Also, we are to be poor in spirit, meaning to empty ourselves and be worldly poor. Job was poor in spirit when he blessed God for taking away everything he had. We must call ourselves poor because we're always in need or want of God's grace, strength, mercy and wisdom. We are so blessed of God because He said, yours is the Kingdom of Heaven. They will obtain the glory of the Kingdom of Heaven. They that mourn here on earth are happy in the end because their trials and troubles are over. Jesus never said how long it was going to take to be happy after we have to mourn and be sorrowful but He did say we would be happy and blessed in the end. The meek shall inherit the earth. This is a temporary gift of God while on earth. When New Jerusalem is brought down from Heaven, the saved and the redeemed shall live here on this refined earth that God has cleaned up from all sin. It will be Heaven on earth and we'll inherit the earth forever. We can have a good life here on earth now even through all of the trials we have to go through. Keep looking up for your redemption draws near. Jesus is coming soon so be ready. Remember, Jesus Christ is the cure for everything. He is the only way.

Chapter 15

The River of Life, the Living Water

Epe.47:1-5, He, God brought me to the door of the house and behold waters were coming out from under the threshold of the temple toward the east for the front of the house stood toward the east. The waters were coming from the south side of the altar. Then He brought me through the north gate and led me around the outer gate facing east and the waters were flowing from the south side. As the man went eastward with a measuring line in his hand he measured off a thousand cubits and He brought me through the waters, the waters were to my ankles. Again he measured a thousand cubits and brought me through the waters, the waters were to my knees. Again he measured a thousand and it was a river that I couldn't pass over for the waters were raised, waters to swim in, and a river that could not be passed over. In verse 1, God was showing him that He was the living water, the Holy Ghost. He is the river of life. He's showing us how we can grow in Him. The Holy Ghost flows from every side to help us in every situation and trial. As we grow in the Lord we get stronger. We come as a little child but we don't have to stay a babe on milk, but as we learn we get on the meat of the Word. The waters were ankle deep. We begin to talk with God at this point. Then the waters were to his knees. Now we need to spend much time on our knees in prayer with God for a deeper relationship with Him and more knowledge of Him. Verse 4, the waters were up to his loins now, or his waist.

When we step into the water this deep then we are showing much growth in the Lord. We're trusting Him more as we grow. We're getting much stronger in the Lord and learning to lean on Him. We have learned more wisdom and we are smarter in the Lord. God said, if you want wisdom then ask Me for it. The world's wisdom is not lasting but God's wisdom will last forever. Now we have more understanding of His Word. In Verse 5, Now the waters were too deep for him to pass over but it was deep enough to swim in. Now we're in the overflow of the Holy Spirit. We're letting the Holy Spirit lead and guide us all the way. We are completely leaning on Him and trusting Him in everything. We have made Spiritual progress. We have to realize that we can do nothing within ourselves. We have to have the Holy Spirit leading, guiding and convicting us to do the right things and live the right way.

Christ is the only source

John 4;10, Jesus answered and said, unto her, if you knew the gift of God and who it is that says to you, Give Me a drink, you would have asked of Him and He would have given you living water. The woman at the well didn't know who Jesus was at that time. John 7:38, They that believes on Me as the scripture has said, out of their belly shall flow rivers of living waters. Jesus satisfies the deepest needs. He is the source for everything. He's all you really need for He will supply your every need and will give you the desire of your heart if you will truly lean on Him. You cannot live without natural water neither can you have eternal life without the Spiritual water, Jesus Christ. Rev.7:7, For the lamb that is in the midst of the throne shall feed them and lead them into living fountains of water and shall wipe away all tears from their eyes. This supply never ends in Heaven. Rev.22:1, And He showed me a pure river of water of life clear as crystal proceeding out of the throne of God and the Lamb. This Lamb is Jesus Christ. In the Old Testament they used lambs for blood sacrifices because a young lamb was without spot or blemish. Jesus gave His blood for us when He died on the cross of Calvary. He became the Lamb for us for He was without spot or blemish.

Universal call to partake

Rev.22:17, And the Spirit and the Bride says come, let them that hear come and they that are thirsty come, and whosoever will, let them take the water of life freely. This is in Heaven now and we are free and we can eat of the tree of life and drink of the living water freely. In Heaven you will be like Christ. We will be Spiritual as He is. We will be like Him the

Bible teaches. We will have no sin or anything that defiles there. In the city of New Jerusalem we shall go in and out as we want. We'll be able to go anywhere in the earth that we want and when we want for it will be like the Garden of Eden, pure and clean. God will have cleaned it up and replenished the whole earth just like He made it in the beginning. There will be no more sin, no more sickness, no more sorrows, no more troubles for it will Heaven on earth. Don't you want to be there? If you want to go there you will have to fulfill these commands from God. You have to live holy here on earth now and follow Jesus all the way.

Gal. 5:16, This I say then, walk in the Spirit and you shall not fulfill the lust of the flesh. You have to die to the flesh in order to walk in the Spirit of God. There's a war that goes on all of the time, the flesh against the Spirit. But you can overcome the flesh with prayer and seeking God. You have to be constant in your walk with the Lord. Epe.4:1, I beseech you, I beg you said Paul, that you walk worthy of the vocation you were called. Your vocation is your new occupation when you were born again. When you came to Jesus, you were saying, I work for You now, for I am on Your payroll. Paul is saying here, walk worthy of that call of Jesus Christ. As you have received Jesus Christ the Lord now walk in Him. Walk circumspectly, careful and cautious, not as fools or sinners but be wise. To walk wise you have to grow spiritual, stronger in the Lord and flourish in Him. You have to be a shining light, for you are now the light of the world and the salt of the earth. You are to let your light shine in the darkness so others can see. You are living in freedom now so live in love for everyone. You have to show mercy to others just as Jesus shows mercy to you. If you want to receive mercy then you will have to give mercy. Job 17:9, The righteous shall hold on to His ways, and they will grow stronger and stronger. This is to hold on to Jesus Christ ways not your way. The righteous go from strength to strength in Christ. David said, they shall flourish like palm trees and grow like a cedar tree in Lebanon. Both of these trees are strong and the palm tree brings forth fruit. We as Christians have to bring forth fruit as well. The fruit of the light consist of all goodness, righteousness, truth and things that please the Lord. The fruit we bring forth is fruit of the Spirit such as joy, peace, love, humility, patience, kindness, goodness, faithfulness, gentleness and self control. Against thee things there is no law. II Cor.3:17, Now the Lord is that Spirit and where the Spirit of the Lord is there is freedom. Abide in faith in Him and grounded in love. Verse 19, To know the love of the Lord you have to be filled with all the fullness of

God. Paul is talking about being baptized in the Holy Spirit in order to have the full knowledge and fullness of God. You need the Holy Spirit to discern between good and bad.

The natural person

I Cor.2:14, The natural person does not know the things of the Spirit of God. The natural person is living by their flesh and the spiritual person is being led by the Holy Spirit. We were all a natural person before we came to Christ. We are still living in the flesh but we are led by the Spirit. A natural person cannot understand the things of God. That's why lots of people cannot understand the Bible. We will never know it all but we will grow stronger and become more knowledgeable as we mature in the Lord. Heb.5:14, Paul said, strong meat belongs to the mature Christian, one who is full of the Spirit and who allows the Holy Spirit to lead them. We are to grow in grace and knowledge of our Lord and Savior Jesus Christ, Amen. Matt. 5:48, Be ye therefore, perfect even as your Father which is in Heaven is perfect. Now we know that there is only one perfect and that is Jesus Christ. But we are to strive to be perfect. We are to always strive to do the things that are pleasing to God. The natural person will never please God for they are still living in the lust of the flesh. The only way they will ever please Him is to repent of their sins and invite Jesus in their heart and follow Him. That's the first step to living a life to please Him. His blood cleanses all from sin. No one has righteousness of their own for our righteousness is as filthy as rags. We are nothing without Jesus in our lives. We have life in the Spirit of God. Rom.8:1, Therefore there is now no condemnation to those who are in Christ Jesus, who walk not after the flesh but after the Spirit. You are not condemned for your past for Jesus has forgiven you if you have repented and accepted Him in your life. He forgives and forgets. Verse 6, To be spiritual minded is life and peace. How deep are you in the waters? You can go as far as you want. You can have as much of God as you want. Remember, the deeper you go in God the stronger you will get. You will have more understanding and wisdom of Him and the brighter your light will shine. The deeper you get in the Lord the more freedom you'll have and the more love you'll have for Him and for others as well. God wants all of you not just a part of you.

God's love is unconditional, our fellowship with Him is not

Ps.66:19-20, God has surely listened and heard our prayers. Praise be to God who has not rejected our prayers or withheld His love from us. When you cry out to Him, He said He would hear and answer as long as you abide in Him. We know the Word has taught us that sin will separate our prayers from Him. For He does not look upon sin. Rom.5; 8, God demonstrated His love for us in this, while we were yet sinners Christ died for us. God knew what this world would be like but He loved us so much that He wanted to try one more time to save us. So He sent His only begotten Son, Jesus to die on the cross and shed His blood for us. That's how much He loves us. It's not His will that any should perish but all come to know Him and have eternal life. If anyone is lost it's by their own choosing. God doesn't make anyone come to Him for everyone has the freedom of choice. The plan has been laid out for you and all you have to do is accept it and follow Him. Rom.8:35-39, Who shall separate us from the love of God? Shall troubles or hardships, shall persecutions, famine, nakedness, danger or sword? No, in all these things we are more than conquerors through Him who loved us. For I am convinced that neither death nor life, neither angels or demons, neither the present or the future nor power, neither heights or depth or anything else in all creation will be able to separate us from the love of God that is in Christ Jesus our Lord. You will never take God's love from you for He will always love you. There is no greater love than for one to lay down their life for another. That's what Jesus did for us. I John 3:1, How great is the love the Father has given us, that we shall be called the children of God.

Our fellowship and love for God is conditional

Isa.59:2, Your iniquities have separated you from God. Your sins have hidden His face from you and He will not hear you. We can separate our love and ourselves from Him. The scripture says, no man can snatch you out of the hand of God meaning, if you are serving and following Him then no one can take you from Him. But you can walk away from Him yourself. We are secure in Him as long as we abide in Him but you decide you no longer want to walk with Him then you separate yourself from Him and you are no longer secure. You have to endure to the end to be saved and secure. There has been so many taught that when you come to Christ and be born again then you are secured for life. The truth of the Scripture does not teach that. You can't live as you want and serve God for you have to die to self and follow Him with your whole heart, mind, soul and strength. You cannot live on yesterday's salvation for today is the day of salvation. No, you don't have to be born again everyday but it's not what you did yesterday but it's what you are doing right now. Yesterday has gone and this is a new day. We are to be renewed everyday in Christ. To be in fellowship with Him you must love Him, be obedient and faithful to Him always. You can't live as the world lives and be one of His children. John 15:7-10, If you <u>remain</u> in Me and My Words <u>remain</u> in you, you shall ask anything and it shall be given you. It's God's glory that you have much fruit showing yourselves that you are My disciples. Jesus said, As My Father has loved Me so I love you, <u>you continue in My love.</u> If you keep My commandments you shall abide in My love, even as I have My Father's commandments and abide in His love. You can see here that you have to continue to abide in Him to have love for Him and have a good relationship with Him. Don't live dangerously and believe that because you were born again that you can live any way you want because this is the trick of the devil. Jesus is coming back for a people who are serving Him with their whole heart and living for Him.

Believers are called to fellowship with Him

I Cor.1:9, God is faithful by whom you were called into the fellowship of His Son Jesus Christ our Lord. He wants to fellowship with you and me. He wants us to talk to Him and enjoy Him. He wants us to tell Him we love Him and how much we need Him and enjoy Him. We will tell Him this one day when we see Him but He wants our fellowship now. John 15:4, Abide in Me and I in you, as the branches cannot bear fruit of itself except it abide in the vine, no more can you except you abide in Me. We have to abide in Him to bear good fruit. Epe.5:2, We are to walk in love as Christ has loved us and given Himself for us. I John 1:6, If we say we have fellowship with Him and walk in darkness we lie and the truth is not in us. God knows your heart and the way you live. It's not what you say but the way you live that really counts. Many confess with their mouth that they know Christ but their lives show different for they are still living the same kind of life as they were before they said they came to Christ. You have to be different after you come to Him. The Bible says that you are a new person for the old person is done away with. I John 1:3, That which we have seen and heard declares that we have fellowship with the Father and His Son Jesus Christ. Verse 7, If we walk in the light as He is in the light we have fellowship one with another and the blood of Jesus Christ cleanses us from all sin. We are to continue in the fellowship with Him and one another. The way you live will show others whether you are living in a manner that you truly are in fellowship with the Lord. We are no one's judge but we are known by the fruit that we bear. If you are unruly, full of anger, rage, bitterness, hatred, envy, malice or living ungodly then it is obvious that you are not following Christ. You can break the fellowship with the Lord and your love for Him. You can see through these scriptures that our love for Him is conditional but His love for us is unconditional. There are rules and commandments that we must follow to stay in love with Him and have fellowship with Him.

We have to do what He has told us

1- We are to keep His commandments

2- Be obedient to Him

3- Our love for Him has to abide in Him

4- We have to love our brothers and sisters

5- We have to walk in the light and not in darkness

6- We can't have sin in our lives

7- We have to love one another

8- We have to abide in Him and He in us

9- His Word has to abide in us

10- We have to endure to the end in Him

God's love for us is unconditional for HE IS LOVE. God never changes, it is us that changes. He will never let go but we can let go of Him. Love is the greatest gift so let's hold on to it forever. The love of God is greater far than any tongue or pen can tell. It's rich and pure and measureless and it shall forevermore endure. His love never dies or goes away and His love never fades. Hold on, for they that endure to the end the same shall be saved.

Chapter 16

We are in a fight

II Tim.4:7, Paul said, I have fought a good fight of faith. I have finished my course and I have kept the faith. He was a winner over all of the obstacles and hard times that he had gone through in this life. He knew it was worth everything that he had to go through to serve Jesus Christ. Now he's ready for the eternal Kingdom of Heaven. We have to finish the course just as Paul did to enter into the Kingdom of Heaven.

We're going to look at the three Fs. fight, finished, and faith. A good fighter is worthy, honorable and noble in the Lord Jesus Christ. We have to fight against self for self is our greatest enemy. Let go and let God so you can overcome the devil and all of his schemes and tricks. He will throw everything he can at you to try to make you fall or fail. He can only do what you allow him to do for greater is He that is in you than he that is in the world. If you have accepted Jesus as Lord of your life then He is living in you.

A good fighter is full of love for God, others and themselves. Love covers a multitude of sin. Love is the greatest gift of all and it never fails for it endures forever. Love doesn't puff up but it builds up. Love is a savory food and gift for it preserves and last forever. Love is better than any banquet or feast. Solomon said, His love is a banner over my head. God's love for His children is like a banner over our heads to comfort and protect us. Song of Solomon 8:6-7, Love is as strong as death and many waters, troubles, sorrows and trials cannot quench love neither floods drown it. Rom.9:28, For all things work together for good to them that love the Lord and are called according to His purpose. Love is like a strong cord that cannot be broken. It takes love to fight a good fight for the Lord in this life and evil generation but God is love and you are a winner in Him.

We have to finish this race to receive a reward. You must keep going to win. You can't stop if you're tired or discouraged. A Christian is compared to a foot race. I Cor.9:24, Know ye not that they which run a race, all run but only one receives the reward. It's a reward that will soon fade away or rust. A Christian is running a race for the crown of life. This reward will never fade away for it will last forever. Paul said that he ran with no uncertainties for he knows he's a winner in the Lord Jesus Christ. He said he didn't box like beating the air but he was striking his adversary the devil. He said, I buffet and keep my body in shape so that after I preach the gospel I will not be looked at as unfit. He said that he took care of his body because it was the temple of God. We are not to do anything with our bodies that is not clean and does not please God. We are to live holy and righteous and not sin. An athlete stays away from everything that will hinder their race to win. We as Christians have to do the same thing. You have to serve Him with your whole heart, mind, soul and strength. He knows your heart and every intent.

Gal. 5:7, Paul said, you did run well but who or what hindered you that you shouldn't obey the truth? Some start this walk with God but go astray, they either quit or fall away. You are to press forward to the mark of the high calling of God for the prize. We are to strip off every weight or sin that so easily besets us or hinders us from doing what we should do in the Lord to win this race for the Lord. We have a lot of witnesses looking at us as well as God. Heb.12:1, Wherefore, seeing that we have compassed about with so great a cloud of witnesses, let us lay aside every weight and sin that does so easily beset us and let us run with patience the race that is set before us. Let us be good witnesses for Him so we can win others to Him. We will be winners in the end.

Be doers of the Word and not just a hearer only. We have to hold fast to the end. Have faith in God and never waver or doubt for to doubt is sin. Without faith you cannot please God and the just shall live by faith. It is by faith that God saved us. Faith will never fail you. Our hearts are purified by faith, we are justified by faith and we are sanctified by faith. Gal.5:6, Faith is activated, energized, expressed and worked through love. Faith and love work together just as faith and works. I Tim.6:12, Fight the good fight of faith, lay hold on eternal life where you are called and have professed a good confession before many witnesses. Verse 14, keep the commandments without spot until the appearing of our Lord Jesus Christ.

What is faith?

Heb.11:1, Faith is the substance of things not seen but are hoped for. If you can see it you don't need faith. You have never seen Jesus but you can see all of His works of creation and you have seen many miracles He has done. If you read the Bible you will read all about Him. The only way you can accept Him is by faith. He is the author and finisher of our faith. He's the author because He saves and He's the finisher because you have to finish in Him. He's the one who holds our future and who holds our hand. He's the author of our faith because He died for our sins so we could have faith in Him and He rose again so we can have eternal life with Him. When you come to Him, then you must do something too. James 2:20, Faith without works is dead. You cannot have faith and have not works too. They go hand in hand and can't be separated, just like you can't separate love from faith. There are a lot of good people but they have no faith. There are many who have faith but have no works. This can't be in the Lord Jesus. When you pray you have to have faith to believer what you pray for is coming to pass. I Pet.1:5, We are kept by the power of God through faith unto salvation ready to be revealed in the last time. Verse 7, That the trial of your faith being much more precious than gold that perishes, though it is tried in the fire might be found unto praise, honor and glory at the appearing of Jesus Christ. You now can rejoice with exceeding great and unspeakable joy and full of glory. Receiving the end of your faith even the salvation of your soul. Faith comes by hearing and hearing by the Word of God.

Faith is a defensive weapon.

Heb.11:6, Without faith it is impossible to please God. For they that come to God must believe that He is and that He does reward the faithful and them that diligently seek Him. Epe.6:16, Above all things, taking the shield of faith where you will be able to quench or dodge the fiery darts of the devil and the wicked. Faith is essential in prayer. We have to ask in faith, believing what we ask we will have. Jesus said, if you believe all thing are possible to them that believe. We are to put on the breast plate of faith and love. They protect our heart and chest. I Tim.1:19, Hold fast to your faith in God and have a good conscience. Some have put away concerning faith and their faith has become ship wrecked. They have lost their way and they have become lost. They are not using their defensive weapon of faith. Heb.10:22, Let us draw near to God with a true heart in full assurance of faith having our hearts separated from all evil and sin, and our bodies washed with pure water. Fight the good fight and finish to the end because of faith and love in God and receive your reward of eternal life. We have a treasure in the Lord Jesus Christ.

The Hidden Treasure

Matt.13:44-48, The Kingdom of Heaven is liken unto treasure hid in the field. When one has found it they go and hide it in the field and then go and sell all they have so to buy the field. It's like a merchant who is seeking a goodly pearl. When he had found it, he went and sold what he had and bought it. Again, the Kingdom Of Heaven is like a net that was cast into the sea for treasure and when it was full it was brought into shore. Then it was search through and all of the bad were thrown out and the good saved. If you see a treasure somewhere you will do all you can to get it. You will be happy when you get it. That's what Heaven is going to be like. It will be nothing but happiness, peace and joy there. You won't have to look for anymore treasure for you will have everything you want and you will be in need for nothing. What a treasure, are you going to be there?

There is going to be a judgment day coming so the good can be separated from the bad. That's what Jesus Christ will do. Verses 49-50, So shall it be in the end when all stand before Christ. The angels shall come forth and sever the wicked from the just and shall cast them into the furnace of fire, there shall be weeping and gnashing of teeth. The righteous and redeemed of God will be able to enter into the Kingdom of God but those who have rejected Christ and were disobedient to Him will be lost forever. The good will be separated from the bad. Jesus is going to make up His jewels. Are you going to be in that group? You have to believe and accept it all by faith. There is a Heaven and a hell. Where are you going to spend eternity?

Seek First the Kingdom

Seek ye first the Kingdom of God and then all of these other things will be added unto you. What things is He talking about? He's talking about all of the blessings that He has in store for you and me and all that follow Him and put Him first in their life. There are all kinds of treasures waiting for you and all kinds of blessings and good things. All of the promises and blessings that are written in the Word of God are for His children. The only promise for the lost is this. If you will come to Me and ask Me into your heart and life I will in no way turn you away. And the other promise is, that if you deny Me then I will deny you before My Father which is in Heaven. One more promise for the lost and all that deny Him is this, there is a hell for all who sinners and evil doers. You do not want to be in this group. Seek the things of God and Heaven and enjoy all of the blessings He has for you.

Matt.13:33, Again the Kingdom of Heaven is liken unto leaven which a woman took and hid in three measures of meal with the whole leavened. This woman put more flour into the dough so she would have more dough for bread. We are to be like the woman, we are to do more for the Kingdom of God so we can have more crowns in Heaven and have more blessing here. We are to seek more lost souls so there will be many saved from the furnace of fire that's coming in the end. We are to grow spiritually. We are to give all to Jesus and not just a little. We are like the rising dough. When we grow in the Lord so everyone will see and know we are different from the world and maybe they too will want what we have in Christ. We should never be satisfied until all the world has been leavened, until there all know the truth of God's Word. When a person has been leavened they rise above the world and the evil that's all around and they will become new. They will become a treasure or jewel for the Lord Jesus Christ. Jesus said, if you will fish for people and catch them then I will clean them.

Spiritual Investments

Matt.6:20, Lay up for yourselves treasures in Heaven where moth or rust will not corrupt and the thieves will not break in and steal. It's only what you do here for the Kingdom of God that's going to count or be of any value. All else is vain for all material things are going to burn up one day. They don't last forever here nor can you carry them with you where you are

155

going. You can't carry them to Heaven or hell. Phil.3:8, Paul said, verily or truly, I count all things to be loss for the excellency of the knowledge of Jesus Christ my Lord, for whom I suffered the loss of everything and I count all them refuge that I may gain Christ. He was saying, nothing compares with Christ for He gave His life for us so we could live. He said, all else is nothing but dung outside of Christ. Paul could have had anything he wanted in this life but he chose to follow Christ and have the hidden treasures that Jesus promised to His children. He wanted to make it into the Kingdom of God and have the greatest treasure of all. David said, riches and honor are with me and they are durable riches and righteousness. The blessings of the Lord makes rich. There are people who make themselves rich in material things but they have nothing without Jesus and are become poor. Jesus Christ is the greatest riches one can ever have. .Christians has the inheritance of Heaven and all of the promises of God. All who follow Him are heirs of the Kingdom of God.

Is your treasure box open?

Prov.28:20, A faithful Christian shall abound with blessings. You will receive all that God has promised. You may be poor in this world's goods but you are rich in Him. Ec.2:26, God gives to those who are good in His sight, wisdom, glory and knowledge. With wisdom and knowledge we will get riches, gold and silver in your treasure box. This kind of gold and silver is of God and will never fade away or rust. Ps.36:8, They will be abundantly satisfied with the fatness of our house and shall drink of the rivers of our pleasures. Jesus said, I have come that they might have life more abundantly here and now, and have life eternal later. We will have abundant grace as well for that is part of the treasures He has for His children. God will make all grace to abound toward us and be sufficiency in all things and we will abound in every good works. God said, He would supply all of our needs according to His riches in glory by Jesus Christ. We are to manage our treasure as God wants us to. We are to be good stewards of our treasure. If your treasure box is open God will fill it for you. But you have to open it, for He won't force it open. Your treasure box is your heart. Open up your heart and let Jesus Christ come in and He will save you, wash you with His blood and forgive you of all your sins. He's the only way to Heaven and to the blessings here on earth. There is no other name on earth, under earth or in Heaven that can save you but Jesus Christ. So open that treasure box and you will never regret it.

Plenty promised

Deut.30:9, The Lord will make you plenteous in every good work of your hands, in the fruit of your body, your cattle and land. He said, I will abundantly bless your provision, I will satisfy the poor with bread. Jesus Christ is the bread of life. I Chr.22:13, You will prosper if you will keep the statues and judgments of the Lord. Be strong and of good courage, dread not or be dismayed. Keep the Words of My covenant and do them and you may prosper in all that you do. In everything you do, do it with all of your heart and you will grow spiritually and physically for God will prosper His children. You have to do something yourselves. You have to keep His commandments and His judgments and you have to do what you do with your whole heart. Don't do things grudgingly, don't dread, grumble or complain about what you have or need to do. If you do it His way then He will bless you abundantly just as He said. If you are a Christian and you are struggling financially then you need to check yourselves. It's not God's fault for He wants all of His children to prosper and have good things. Are you giving your 10% to God as He requires you to do? He said to bring all of your tithes and offerings into His storehouse. Until after you have tithes you have not given anything for that belong to Him, it's not yours. This could be your problem and why you aren't prospering if you are having problems financially. You have to keep God's commands to receive all of the blessings that He has for you. Ps.23:5-6, Thou has prepared a table before me in the presence of my enemies. You anointed my head with oil and my cup runs over. Surely goodness and mercy will follow me all the days of my life and I will dwell in the house of the Lord forever. How great God's goodness and mercies are for His children. He has promised all of these good things to all who will follow Him, who fear Him and for all who trust in Him.

Our glorious inheritance

Matt.25:34, Come ye, blessed of My Father, inherit the Kingdom prepared for you from the foundation of the world. He never meant for the world to get in the mess it's in today. He made Heaven right here on earth to begin with. That was His intentions for all people but Adam and Eve sinned and messed it all up. He is still preparing another Heaven for His children. God made another way for us when He gave His only begotten Son, Jesus

Christ to come to die on the cross and then rise the third day and then was received up into Heaven where He's sitting at the right hand of the Father interceding for you and me. So He has provide Heaven for all who will accept Him and follow Him all of the way and will endure to the end. Everyone is invited but you have to accept the invitation. Just as if you were invited to someone's place here on earth you would have the choice to accept or reject the invitation. It's each one's choice, but why would anyone want to miss out on such an invitation as this one? It's the greatest place you can ever go for it will all be peace, joy and happiness there. He's preparing all a mansion there. There will be streets paved with gold, walls of jasper and everything will be beautiful with no flaws anyplace. There will be a river of life flowing freely and a tree with all kind of fruits growing on it. We just can't imagine how beautiful it's going to be. And most of all, Jesus Christ will be there and this home will be eternal. You just don't want to miss this eternal home. You have to prepare here on this earth to go there. After death here you will not have another chance to prepare for you have then chosen where you are going, Heaven or hell. Where are your treasures laid up? Where your heart is that's where your treasure is. Someone has said, wherever you spend your money is where your treasure is, and I quote. You have to deposit something into the Kingdom of God to get something. That's why Jesus said, Lay up your treasures in Heaven. You came here with nothing and you will carry nothing with you when you die. All you will have is the treasure that you have laid up in the Kingdom of God. How full is your luggage of good works for the Kingdom?

Heaven is our Home, not earth

The world is not my home I'm just passing through. My treasures are laid up somewhere beyond the blue. The angels beckoned me from Heaven's opened door, and I can't feel at home in this world anymore. We are just pilgrims here passing through so don't lay down deep roots or stakes here. We're going to move to a better place soon. Don't just live for the moment but live for the duration. Live your life here in a manner that pleases God so you can live eternally with Him in His Kingdom .There's nothing here worth losing your inheritance in Heaven for. Luke 14:38, Whosoever forsakes not all that they have cannot be My disciple. The only thing that you will have in this life is what you give away. Give Jesus to everyone and you will have life. It isn't love until you give it away. Jesus said, When you give to others you are giving to Me. When you give you are laying up treasures in Heaven. Mortify your members of all things that are not godly such as fornication, uncleanness, evil affections, covetousness, idolatry and every evil way and you will have life. Deny yourself of everything for the cause of Christ. Give and you will receive for it is better to give than to receive. God loves a cheerful giver. Give to it feels good. The only path to receiving is giving. The Bible is our road map and Jesus has shown us the way to Heaven. We can't get there by doing our way but we have to do it His way. As I have said before, there's only one way to Heaven and that's through Jesus Christ.

Growth of the Kingdom

Matt.24:14, The gospel of the Kingdom shall be preached to all of the world for a witness unto all nations and then the end shall come. We are to tell the gospel to all we see and then send to other nations the gospel so they will know and come to Him. Declare His glory to all people. Make sure your whole household is saved and on the way to Heaven. All that are saved have crucified themselves of all affections of the lust of the flesh and all evil ways. You are living after the Spirit now, this is the growth of the Kingdom. The growth of the Kingdom is like a handful of corn when it is sown and then it flourishes with so much more when it comes up. We are to tell the gospel to everyone and see the Kingdom grow. You can't make a person accept the Word but you have to tell it so their blood won't be on your hands. Our commission is that we tell the whole world about Jesus Christ. It is God's will that no one perish but all have everlasting life.

Go and My presence goes with you

Ex.4:12, Go and I will be with your mouth and I will teach you what you shall say. Isaiah 51:16, I have put words in your mouth and I have covered you in the shadow of My hands. Jer.5:14, The Lord said, because you speak My Word, I will make My Words in your mouth fire. Paul said, I don't speak words of man's wisdom but what the Holy Ghost teaches, comparing Spiritual things with Spiritual. There is a Spirit in man and the inspiration of the Almighty gives them understanding. Don't be afraid to speak or tell about Jesus. Perfect love casts out all fear. We have the love of God in us and we are to pass it on to others to get all we can into the Kingdom of God as we can so they can find all of the treasures and blessings of the Lord Jesus Christ. No other treasure will ever compare to Him. We have this treasure inside of us, the Holy Spirit. Jesus is living within you and me for we are the children of God.

Have you stopped looking for Jesus?

Ps.123:2, Behold the eyes of the servants look to their masters and the eyes of the maiden look to her mistress, so our eyes look to the Lord our God. David said, I look and I lift up my eyes to You Lord. He kept looking and seeking for God for He knew God was his righteousness. He said, I look for the Lord and He heard me and He delivered me from all my fears. When we look for Jesus we will find Him and be enlightened for He is our joy and strength. We are to turn our eyes upon Him. If you look for Him you will find Him. God said, Look to Me and you will be saved. Look for Jesus for there is redemption in Him. I John1:4, The disciples had seen Jesus and they have experienced him, so they are telling the world to anyone who will listen or heed to them. That which was in the beginning which we have heard and seen with our own eyes and we have looked upon and our hands has touched, the Word of life. Jesus is the Word, He is the light of the world. His life has manifested to us and we have seen it and bear witness and we show you that eternal life which was with the Father and was manifested unto us. That which we have seen and heard we declare unto you that you have this fellowship with us and with the Father and His Son Jesus Christ. We write this so that your joy shall be full.

John 1:36-39, And looking unto Jesus as John walked he said, behold the Lamb of God. Two of John's disciples heard John speak and they too followed Jesus. Jesus turned to them and asked, whom do you seek or who are you looking for? They said, we are looking for the Rabbi, which is to say, Master. They asked Jesus, where do You live? Jesus said, come and see. They went and stayed with Jesus that day. Verse 41, The disciples said, we have found the Messiah, we have found Christ. They were looking for Him and they found Him. You can find Him too if you are looking for Him. You have to seek Him with all of your heart, mind, soul and strength. Call on and He will answer.

Matt.28:1-8, Mary Magdalene and the other Mary went to see the tomb where Jesus was laid. An angel rolled back the stone and said, fear not for I know you seek Jesus. He is not here for He has risen. Go tell His disciples. You will find Him in Galilee. They went quickly because they wanted to see Jesus. They went looking and they found Him just where the angel said He would be. He's always where you can find Him for He is not lost. Luke 4:40-42, When Jesus was preaching, teaching and healing in Capernaum, He healed all of the sick and cast out devils in people. When day came he departed and went into a deserted place. But the people sought Him, they came and stayed with Him so He could not leave them. They didn't want to get out of His presence. Have you even been in that position that you didn't want to move or go anywhere because you wanted to stay in His presence? I have and it's the most wonderful place to ever be. There is such peace and comfort in His presence. When you are in His presence you feel for it's just you and the Lord. You feel no pain, sorrow or any weight of the world. You are in His complete power and presence. Oh, what a place to be.

Luke 19:1-4, There was a little man Zacchaeus in Jericho. He was a very rich publican, he was chief among the publicans. He sought Jesus, he was looking for Him. He was a short man in statue so he climbed up in a tree so he could see him as He passed by. People that want to see Jesus will do anything they can to see Him. You can't see Him through your physical eyes but you can see Him spiritually. Verse 5, Jesus told him to come down out of the tree for He was going home with him and abide in his house today. Jesus will come and abide in your house also if your heart is yearning for Him. Today is the day of salvation and Jesus is our salvation. If you are lost you need to look for Him and if you look you will find Him for He is not lost but you are.

Looking for self gain

John 4:22-27, After the event of Jesus feeding the five thousand the people saw Jesus on the other side. They found a boat and went to the other side of the sea looking for Him. They were following Him for all of the wrong reasons. They were following him for worldly motives and self desires. Jesus said to them, you seek me because you saw me do miracles. Because you were gained from the miracle you want more. You wanted the bread and the fish and you were filled and satisfied. He told them not to work for food that perishes but for the meat that endures forever, everlasting life which the Son of man Jesus Christ shall give. There are people today that just want to find Him for their earthly pleasure and just when they need something from Him. This is what He was telling these people there. He knows your heart and your motive whether you want Him because you love Him and want to follow Him or just for self gain. He wants to meet your needs and He will but He wants your whole heart and life. Look for Him because you love Him. He knows your needs and desires before you ask Him and if you will be true to Him He will meet all of your needs and give you the desire of your heart.

Titus 2:13-14, We are to live righteous and godly in this present world. We are to be looking for that blessed hope and the glorious appearing of our Lord and Savior Jesus Christ. He said He was coming back for those who are looking for Him. Are you looking and earnestly desiring for Jesus to come? There's coming a day when we will see Him face to face in all of His glory. In the back of the Bible, Rev. 22: 20, We are to pray, even so come Lord Jesus. I used to say, Lord don't come yet, for all of my children are not in. Now I not only have to be concerned for my children, but for my grandchildren and great grandchildren. But I want to see Him and I'm tired of what's going on in this world. I believe we need to do all things that He has said not just some of them. Jesus said in this verse, I come quickly and John said, even so come, Lord Jesus. John was anxious for Him to come way back then. Are you looking for Him? Are you praying for Him to come? Rev.8:13, And they shall see Him face to face and His name shall be written in their forehead. Verse 7, behold, I come quickly, blessed are they that keep the prophecy of this book, the Bible. Verse 12, Behold, I come quickly and My reward is with Me to give everyone according to their work. Blessed are they that keep My commandments.

Who are you following?

Are you following the flesh? If you are then you will die. Your flesh will cause you to do all kinds of evil and sins. It will cause you to lust after sinful things, immoralities, envy, hate, evil speaking, and anything that is not of God. In order to follow Christ you have to die to flesh daily and pick up your cross and follow Him all of the way unto the end. Are you following your family? Luke 18:29, Jesus said, Verily I say unto you, there is no one that has left home, parents, brothers, wife or children for the Kingdom's sake, who shall not receive manifold more in this present world and in the world to come. Peter said that they had left all to follow Christ. Are you following the world? Jesus said, I am the light of the world, whosoever will follow Me shall not walk in darkness. The world walks in darkness because they don't know the Light. James 4:4 whoever is a friend to the world is an enemy of God. I John 2:15, Love not the world nor what's in the world. If any man loves the world then the love of the Father is not in Him. Verse 17, The world passes away and the lusts thereof, but they that does the will of God abides forever. Gal.5:16-17, Follow Jesus and walk in the Spirit and you will not fulfill the lust of the flesh. The flesh wars against the Spirit. Let God lead and guide you all the way. Let nothing come between you and serving Him. Don't let anyone or anything become a stumbling block to you and cause you to stop following Jesus. Be careful not to follow false teachers or any kind of idols.

Rewards for Jesus followers

Hosea 6:13, If we follow on to know the Lord, He has prepared for His children to rain down the rain and the latter rain. He rains blessings down on His children now but He's going to rain down the latter rain as well. The latter rain is eternal life. John 10:27, My sheep know My voice and they follow Me. If you are Mine and serve Me, where I am you shall be also. Rejoice and be exceedingly glad for great is your reward in Heaven. You have in Heaven a better and enduring substance. We will have no problems, sicknesses, pain, death or any other troubles for they will all be over. There will be happiness, joy, peace and everything good. II Tim.4:8, Therefore is laid up for me a crown of righteousness, which the Lord the righteous judge shall give at that day, not only to me but to all who love His appearing. James 1:12, Blessed are they that endure temptations for when they are tried they shall retain the crown of life, which the Lord has promised to all that love Him. You shall receive a crown of glory that will never fade away. Hold on to what you have in the Lord and don't let anyone steal your crown. Be sure you endure to the end, the same shall be saved. Hosea 10:12, Sow to yourselves in righteousness, reap in mercy, break up your fallow ground. For it is time to seek the Lord until He comes and rain down righteousness on you. Shake up that part of you that's not in line with His will and do away with it. Search your heart to see if there is anything that's not lining up with His Word. We do have to check ourselves often. He's coming back after a church without spot or wrinkle so we need to make sure everything's all right in His eyes.

Chapter 17

You Are a Slave to Whom You Serve

Rom.6; 16-18, Know ye not that whom you yield yourselves servants to obey, you are the servant to the one you obey. Whether sin unto death or of obedience unto righteousness. But to God be thankful that you once were a servant of sin but you now obey from the heart the form of doctrine that was delivered you. Being made from sin, you became a servant of righteousness. Verse 22, now being made free from sin and become servants of God, you have your fruits unto holiness and the end everlasting life. For the wages of sin is death but the gift of God is eternal life through Jesus Christ our Lord. Before you were born again you are a servant to sin and the devil. You were a slave to many things that were evil and wrong. You can still be slave to things after you are born again. Lots are people are slaves to TV. Some are slaves to their work. Some are even slaves to food. They don't have to be sin to be a slave to. What ever you take too much time in can be your slave. Whatever possesses you causes you to be a slave to it. Of course, you can become slaves to people. There are some who will just use you to get what they want. Its one thing to help someone but it's another things to be used by them. I don't believe that God wants that to happen to His children.

We are to be servants of God

I Cor.7:23, You know you were bought with a price so we don't have to be servants to man. Verse 22, For they that are called in the Lord, being a servant, is the Lord's free ones. Likewise, they that are called being free are Christ's servants. Therefore, you are to abide with God. We are to please God in all things. We are servants to Him because we love Him and want to do all that we know pleases Him and do keep all of His commands. To be a servant to Him is an honor. Rom. 8:14 and 17, For as many that are led by the Spirit of God are the sons and daughters of God. If children of God then you are heirs of Him and joint heirs with Christ, being justified by His grace. We have been made heirs according to the hope of eternal life. Once you are saved then you are not to entangle yourself again to the world and sin. You are free in Christ Jesus but don't allow yourself to be in bondage or slavery again. Whoever commits sin is a servant to sin. Jesus has set you free from sin when He saves you then you can live above sin. For greater is He that is in you than he that is in the world. Don't let the cares of this world and the deceitful things, riches or lusts come back to you and into your heart. Sin will choke out the Word of God that's in you. The Holy Spirit will not live in a temple that's full of sin. Stay free in the Lord Jesus Christ our Savior.

I Cor.10:12-13, Take heed lest you fall. When you think you stand strong, be careful lest you be tempted and fall. There has no temptation taken you but such as is common to man. But God is faithful who will not suffer you to be tempted above what you are able to stand or resist. But with the temptation, He will make a way to escape that you may be able to bear. I have just learned something that I have never seen before. I have always heard others preach that God will make a way for you escape all of your temptations. But that's not what He said. He said that He would make a way for you to escape anymore than you can bear. May God forgive me for telling the wrong thing to others. We have to go through trials and tribulations all of the days of our lives if we follow Him. He said He would make a way so we can bear what ever we have to go through. Acts 14:22, We must go through many tribulations here on this earth to enter into the Kingdom of God. John 16:33, In this world you shall have tribulations but be of good cheer for I have overcome the world. Tribulations are a part of afflictions but remember, God is always with you.

Way Provided

Through the difficulties of life's journey, God will make a way for His children. Ex.14:16, When Moses led the children of Israel out of Egypt and came to the Red Sea and the army of Egypt was coming behind them to kill them, God made a way for them to escape. He told Moses to stretch forth his rod and stretch out his hand over the sea and divide it. It was divided and the sea rolled back for them to cross over on dry land. They didn't even get their feet wet for the Lord kept the land dry. You know the rest of the story. The Egyptians saw them and they started to cross behind them but God rolled back the waters and they all were drowned. God will make a way where there seem to be none. All you have to do is trust and obey Him. Prov.15:19, The way of the righteous is made plain. We are to walk in the way God leads us. God said, I will make the dark places light, and the crooked things straight for you. I will not forsake you. Heb.13:6, The Lord is my helper and I will not fear what anyone shall do unto me. Ps.28:7, The Lord is my strength and shield my heart trust in Him and I am helped. My heart greatly rejoices and with my song I will praise Him. God is my deliverer, my healer, my salvation, my keeper, my strength and my all. He has made so many ways for me. In my trials and troubles He has given me strength to go through all of them. When I thought that I just couldn't go on, He made a way and was there with me. Many times He has sent someone to encourage or give me a word to lift me up. He has truly let me know that He will never leave or forsake me. I am what I am today because of Jesus Christ and His love and mercy. It's because of His love and mercy that I am still living still.

Before my first husband died I though that he was going to kill me. He was an alcoholic and loved his women. He would go out at nights come home all drunk up and accuse me of doing something wrong, when all of the time I was right at home with my four girls. He would hit me and I would run and fall down trying to get away from him. I fell down one time and ended up with blood clots in my knee and leg, oh that was so painful. I am still wearing scars today from some of those times. I just knew that he would kill me one day but God was with me and kept His hand upon me. He died at an early age because of sin of not following Jesus Christ. I never wished him to die but I wondered how I was going to stand much more. It was so bad I left him several times but for the children's sake I would go back praying he would change but he never did for he only got worse. I don't know whether he had time to repent or not before he died, only God knows. My girls have told me many times that they believe God took him so I would live and take care of them. That could be true, all I know is God did take good care of me and the girls. I'll always believe that God spared my life when He took him. I am telling you this in hopes that it helps someone else. When things look like there is no way out just look to Jesus Christ for He will make a way for you. I can truly say with Paul, the Lord is my helper I will not fear what man can do to me.

God gives us power.

Luke 10:19, Behold I give unto you, power to tread over serpents and scorpions and over all the power of the enemy and nothing by any means will hurt you. Jesus told Peter that the devil wanted to sift him as wheat, but I have prayed for you that your faith will not fail. Do you know that Jesus is still praying to the Father for His children today? You can read this in John 17. God said, He was going to bruise the devil under our feet shortly. Jesus Himself was tested and suffered. We have the power in Jesus name to come against the devil and his evil forces only in the name of Jesus. We have no power in ourselves but in His name. The devil's power is no match to our Lord Jesus Christ power. Jesus is still praying for His children today but not for the world. If you have Jesus then you have everything. Without Him you can do nothing. He gives you the strength and breath to get out of bed everyday. He gives you power to do what you have to do everyday. Don't ever take anything for granite for it's Him who keeps you going and alive. Remember, we've got the power in the name of Jesus.

Gain through loss

You may lose earthly goods for serving Jesus Christ but you will gain eternal life if you follow Him all of the way to the end. If you take some of your treasure and give to the poor and needy then you will gain for you're laying up treasures in Heaven. When you sacrifice your family, friends, children and properties then you shall receive a hundred fold here and inherit everlasting life. That doesn't mean that you literally desert them but you give God first place in your heart and life. Mark 8:35, For whosoever will save his life shall lose it but, whosoever will lose his life for My sake and the gospel shall save it. Life comes out of death. When you die to self and live for Christ then you will have eternal life. It's like a grain of corn. When you plant it, it has to die to live and bring forth more corn. This is compared to Christians. Unless we die to self we cannot be fruitful to Christ and will not have everlasting life in the Kingdom of God. Paul gave up everything to follow Christ. He said, everything else was loss he counted as dung. It's only what you do for Christ here that will count and endure. John 12;26, If anyone serve Me, let them follow Me and where I am you may be there also, and My father will honor them. When you follow Christ, He will lead you down the path that leads you to the

Kingdom of God. Whosoever believes and lives in Jesus Christ will never die. You will just fall asleep and wake up with Him. How wonderful to know this. Jesus told this to Martha when her brother Lazarus died. He proved what He said was true. When Jesus called him out of the tomb and said, Lazarus, come forth, he came out still wrapped in the grave clothes and Jesus told him to take them off. You will live again if you die in Christ. We will gain it all through death. Jesus said that He knew His children by their name and they will never perish again. I am so glad that He knows my name and I will always love and praise Him.

The inseparable Christ

Matt. 28:20. Teach them to do all things and whatsoever I have commanded you and lo I am with you always, even to the end of the world. I gave them eternal life and they shall never perish again, neither will any man pluck them out of My hand. Abide in Me and I in you. We have to stay in Him always. Just like a branch cannot bear fruit unless it stays on the vine. The vine is Christ and we are the branches. There is no power that can separate God's love from us for He is love. We can allow things or people to separate our love from Him but no one can take His love for us away. He loves you with an everlasting love and He is faithful to keep His Word. I John 4:16, And we have known the love that God has shown to us. God is love and they that dwell in love dwells in Him and He in them. God will never separate Himself from you as long as you abide in Him. You may not feel Him at times but He is still there with you. He may not give you the things that you ask for when you ask for them but He hears you and will answer at the right time when it's best for you. Do you believe this? You have to believe His Word and not doubt to receive anything from Him.

Your labor is not in vain

I Cor.15;58, Paul said, Therefore my beloved brethren, be ye steadfast, unmovable always abounding in the work of the Lord, for as much as you know that your labor is not in vain in the Lord. Jesus said, that whosoever will give a cup of water in My name because you love Me and belong to Me, truly I say unto you, you shall not lose your reward. It's doesn't matter what you do as long as you do it unto the Lord Jesus Christ and in His name. Rom.2:10, Glory, honor and peace to everyone that works for the good. You may feel you are doing nothing but if you are spreading joy of the Lord, you have a ministry. You can reach out to people just by encouraging them and being friendly to them. Showing people love is one of the greatest things you can do. You will never know how many people you have brought to the Lord until we get to Heaven and sit down and talk to Jesus. We all have a ministry and a work for the Lord. I Cor.3:14, If anyone's work abide which they have built upon, they shall receive a reward. You have to continue to work and not quit. It's like a job, you have to work so many years or until you're old enough to retire to get a pension and retirement pay. If you quit too early, then you will lose all of that. Same way in the Lord's work, you have to continue to the end. You have to have faith to please God but you also have to have works with faith, faith without works is dead. You can't get to Heaven with just your works for you have to have faith. Remember there is no room for doubt in a Christian's life. If you doubt you will receive nothing. There is no wages on earth that's compare to the wages in God's work. Nothing here will give you eternal life or will give you the benefits that God gives. His benefits are secure and everlasting.

Chapter 18

Sin Begins In the Thoughts of Your Mind

Mark 7:20-23, Jesus said. That which comes out of a person's mouth defiles them. For within the heart comes a person's thoughts. Adultery, fornication, murders, thefts, covetous, wickedness, lasciviousness evil eyes, blasphemy, pride and foolishness. All of these things come from within a person. You can have control over all of these sinful things. You can have control over your thoughts and over the mind by keeping your mind on Jesus and the good things of Him. We have the mind of Christ if you have been born again and have Him living within you.

Rom.12:2, Be not conformed to this world but be ye transformed by the renewing of your mind, that you may prove what is good and acceptable and perfect will of God. Our minds are renewed when we are born again. We are not to follow the world but to follow Him. The world and the things of the world are evil and is lead by the devil. You never want to go back to the world after you are born again in Jesus Christ. God will help you renew your mind daily. If you desire to follow the world then He will let you for you are free to serve whom you want. He doesn't make anyone follow Him for it's each one's choice. Rom. 1:28, God gave them over to a reprobate mind to do the things which are not convenient or good. These men were evil and wouldn't listen to what was good so God gave them up to do what they wanted to do. He will do the same today if you choose not to follow Jesus Christ. He wants you to serve Him and do good but He doesn't make you. There are only two ways to go and that's God's way or the devil's way, which is the world's way. He is the father of darkness and hell in the end. Jesus is the light of the world and He wants you to overcome the devil and his ways and come follow Him. II Cor.10:5,

We are to cast down every imagination and the bad thoughts that are not in line with the will of God. We are to bring captivity or every thought that is not of God and bring your thoughts and mind unto the obedience of God. Keep your mind and thoughts under subjection to God. Phil.2:5, Let this mind be in you which was also in Christ Jesus. Epe.4:23-27, Be renewed in the Spirit of your mind. Put on a new you which after God has created in righteousness and holiness. Put away all lying and speak truth to everyone. Be ye angry but sin not, don't let the sun go down on your wrath, neither give place to the devil. Verses 29- 30, Let no evil or corrupt conversation come out of your mouth but what is good and edifying, that it will minister grace to all hearers. Be honest with everyone, let your yes be yes and your no be no. Live in a manner that everyone can trust you. Have the love of God working in you and don't let the devil tempt you into doing or thinking evil things and then committing them. Sin starts in the thoughts of your mind and when you dwell on them they become reality. Do away with the bad thoughts before they become action. Don't grieve the Holy Spirit of God whereby you have been sealed unto the day of redemption. Verses 31-32, Let all bitterness, anger, clamor and all evil speaking be put away from you, along with all malice also. Be kind to one another, tender hearted, forgiving one another, even as God for Christ sake forgave you. Be followers of God and walk in His ways and you will be able to control your mind and thoughts and bring them all under the subjection of Jesus Christ. Your mind and thoughts have to be in submission to God, just as a wife has to be in submission to her husband in Christ Jesus.

Phil.4:6-8, Be careful in nothing but in everything with prayer and supplication with thanksgiving. Let your requests be known unto God. And the peace of God that passes all understanding shall keep your hearts and minds through Jesus Christ. Finally brethren, whatever things are true, honest, just, pure, and lovely, of good report, any virtue and praise, think on these things. We don't have to fret ourselves over anything but ask God for what we need and He will supply them. Always be thankful in everything not for everything such as problems and troubles but, be thankful in everything knowing that God is in control. He will work it all out if we will just be obedient and follow Him. Worry is sin. You can be concerned about something but not worry. If you are worrying about something then you're not putting it into God's hands. James has told you that if you doubt you are like the waves on the sea tossed to and fro and you will receive nothing from God. You have to trust Him with all of your heart, mind, soul and strength. To doubt is a terrible thing. To doubt means that you're not trusting. This makes a miserable life. Doubt will lead to death and hell in the end. You can't have doubt and faith at the same time. Faith pleases God and the just shall live by faith, so do not doubt God.

God's thoughts of you

Isa.26:3-4, God will keep them in perfect peace whose mind is stayed on Him, because they trust in Him. Trust in the Lord forever for the Lord Jehovah is everlasting strength. Jer.29:11-13, Our God said these words to Jeremiah the prophet and it still stands today for He and His Word never changes. For I know the thoughts that I think of you says the Lord. Thoughts of peace and not evil, to give you an expected end. Do you expect a good end? God is saying, whatever you are expecting I will give you in the end. He has a plan for everyone and it's up to each individual to keep His plan. He has a great expected end for all who will trust Him, be obedient, serve Him and walk in His will. You can know what your expected end is. If you are living the life for Him then your end will be eternal life. If not, then your end will be a bad one, eternal hell. God knows which one it will be. It is God's will that all would have His expected end for it is His will that none shall perish but all have eternal life. Which will it be Heaven or hell? He said you can call on Him at anytime and He will hear and answer you. You shall seek Me and you will find Me, when you search for Me with your whole heart. Keep your thoughts and mind on Him for He keeps His mind and thoughts on you.

Wise thoughts

Ps.48:9, David said, we have thoughts of loving kindness O God. The thoughts of the righteous are right. We are to think soberly according as God has dealt with every person the measure of faith. All Christians have a certain measure of faith. The closer to God you get the more faith you will have because you know Him and you trust Him more. A good relationship with Him gives you more peace, comfort and strength. David said, My delight is in the law of the Lord and in Him does he meditate day and night. He thinks of Him day and night. He's wise because he keeps his mind and thoughts on God. Ps.77:11-12, I will remember the works of the Lord, surely I will remember Thy wonders of old. I will meditate also of all the works and talk of thy doings. David was saying, I will never forget all of your works. He said that his thoughts of Him were sweet and he was glad and happy in the Lord. If you will keep your minds on Him and the good things He has done then it will overcome the bad things. Even in the bad times there have been good things to come out of them. God is good. He can deliver you from any bad thoughts in your mind. He did it for me and I know He will do it for you. You should never dwell on your past, especially if you have had a bad one. Bad thoughts can cause depression, oppression and even sickness in your body. Give it to God and let Him wipe away all bad thoughts from your mind.

I have been ministering to a sweet little lady from my church. She had a bad childhood along with a broken marriage. Every time anyone would talk to her she would only talk about her past. She does have a lot of hurt and she can't seem to get over it or forget it. She has been in and out of the mental hospital because of this. All they do is give her more medication. I have given her scripture after scripture, prayed with her and encouraged her to give it to God for it is too big for her to handle. Only He can take away the thoughts of these kinds of hurts. I know, because God did it for me. I was carrying such a load of bad thoughts that it kept bringing me down. There comes a time when you have to realize that there are some things that a person just can't handle themselves. You can't change the past so the best thing is to move on and ask God to wipe away the thoughts. My dad always said and I quote, why worry over things that you can't change or do anything about? God took all of the bad thoughts away and let me remember the good things. My dad also said, no one is all bad, for there is something good is everyone. I found this to be true for I was able to remember some good things and I didn't think on the bad. Only God can do that. Remembering your bad past can cause a person their life. Many people have taken their life because of their thoughts. It has just about destroyed this lady. I haven't seen her in church for a good while now. The last I heard she was still in and out of the hospital. I know that God uses doctors and medication but Jesus Christ is the great Physician and we need to lean and trust in Him. If she would just let go and trust God I know He would help her and heal her of this problem. I can say this from experience. I never talk about my past because He took the memories away, praise His Holy name. Many people have been destroyed because of their thoughts. Many times what a person thinks isn't even true. Many people worry about things that never happen. You need to renew your mind daily in the Lord. Rom.8:7, The carnal mind is an enemy against God for it is not committed to the laws of God and it can't be. You can't walk according to your mind and walk in God at the same time. Prov.23:7, For as a person thinks in their heart so it is. Prov.24:9, The thoughts of foolishness is sin. Matt.9:4, Jesus knows your every thought. When you will not listen to God and you are determined to do it your way, you have a carnal mind. When you do not listen to God it makes you become carnal. To be carnal you are being disobedient to Him and you are doing it your way. If you lack wisdom you must pray and ask God and He will make you wise and your thought will be wise also.

Consider the end

Deut.32:29, Moses said, if you were wise and understood, you would consider your latter end. If you can just think of what your end is going to be, you would have wise thoughts. If you have given your all to Jesus then you will have a blessed end. If you have not then your end is going to be worse than you have ever seen or even can imagine. If you could see just how bad it will be without Christ in your life I believe everyone would live a better life and be ready to leave this place here. If you could see the bad end I believe you would do everything to bring your mind as well as your body under the subjection of Jesus Christ. Just think about it, what is your latter end going to be and where? Be wise like Moses has said and consider your latter end. You can have a perfect end in Christ.

Our body is the temple of God

I Cor.3:16-17, Know ye not that your body is the temple of God and that the Spirit of God lives in you? If anyone defiles the temple of God then shall God destroy it for the temple of God is holy. Which temple are you? Is Jesus living in you? If you have accepted Him as your Lord and Savior and you are serving Him, then He is living in you. You are to keep your body under subjection to Him, live holy and righteous. Rom.12:1, I beg you therefore brethren by the mercies of God that you present your bodies a living sacrifice, holy and acceptable unto God, which is your reasonable service. We are not to do or allow anything to harm our bodies in any way. Like our minds that we have just talked about, it's a big part of our body for it controls our ways. II Cor.4:7, We have this treasure in earthen vessels that the excellency of the power may be of God and not of us. We are not ours for we were bought with a price. Jesus gave His life on the cross at Calvary. We are not to do whatever we want but whatever says the Word of the Lord. He is living in us so we are to be living for Him and in Him. We are to live holy for He is holy. As obedient children we are not to fashion ourselves as we once did but be holy in all manner of conversations and doings. If you are living in Him then you want the things of God.

Ex. 20:9-10, Six days shall you labor and do all your work, but on the seventh day you should rest for this is the Sabbath day of the Lord. Verse 11, For God made Heaven and earth in six days and He rested on the seventh day. God blessed this day and He hallowed it. It is to be kept holy unto the Lord. We are to rest on the seventh day so our bodies won't get broken down. Many people, even Christians over work their bodies. You are not taking care of your temple when you over work. If it wasn't important then God would not have blessed and hallowed this seventh day unto Him. He knows that our bodies need a rest from labor. You can over work as easy as you can over eat which abuses your body also. Even God rested on the seventh day so we are to follow His example. He will never lead us astray or down the wrong path. He knows what's good for us and we are to follow. Again, people allow their thoughts to rule them by telling them they have to work seven days a week. They say, we don't have time to rest. If you make yourself sick from over work then you won't be able to work at all. So do it God's way and you will win in the end. There's victory in Jesus Christ. Don't let the thoughts of your mind cause you to sin.

Chapter 19

Replace Doubt for Faith

The enemy of faith is doubt. You need to replace doubt for faith. For doubt and faith does not go together. You will have one or the other. There's no room for doubt in faith. To doubt the things of God is sin. The just shall live by faith and without faith you cannot please God. Everyone has faith in something for you wouldn't even get out of bed if you didn't have faith that you could stand. When you are sitting you have faith when you get up that your legs are going to work for you. When you go to start your car you have faith that it's going to start and to take you and bring you back from where you want to go. There are many things that you have faith in so why can't you have faith in God? You can't see Him you may say. But you can't see your car running before you start it either. You can't see yourself walking before you take the first step but you have faith that you will walk. That's how it is with faith in God. You've never seen Him but you have seen His work of His creation and you have heard of the miracles that He has done. You are a miracle yourself for you were born of your mother. The birth of a baby is a miracle of God. He said to test, try and prove Me that I won't do the things that I said I would do. You can't tempt Him but you should try Him for He will never fail you. He will prove to you that He is who He says He is. He is the Great I Am, the Almighty God the creator of all things and He loves you.

Faith and doubt is a choice. You can choose which it will be. Rom.10:17, Faith comes by hearing and hearing by the Word of God. Get in the Word of God, the Bible and He will reveal Himself to you. You have to accept Him by faith and faith alone. Faith is a gift of God. It is by faith that you are born again and your sins all washed away. You then have to live by faith. Faith is not something you can see for if you can see it you don't need faith. Faith is the substance of things hoped for and the things not seen. If you don't have faith in God then you are denying Him and if you deny Him then you are lost forever.

Don't let doubt come into your heart and life after you have accepted Jesus as your Lord and Savior. Like I said, to doubt is to sin. You need to stay among positive and Christian people. If you are around doubters then you will be tempted to doubt. You are either going to bring them up to your level and what you believe or they will carry you down to theirs. Be careful for the flesh is weak but God is strong. To doubt is of the flesh but faith is of the Spirit and of God. Always remember that greater is He that is in you than he that is in the world. God is in you but the devil is in the world. You have power in Jesus name to come against the devil. Draw near to God and He will draw near to you, resist the devil and he will flee from you. The devil is not afraid of you but he is afraid of the name of Jesus for he knows the power of the Lord. Pray and ask God to help you in your weaknesses and give you more faith. Pray that He will help you in your unbelief. We all have our weaknesses and God knows what they are and if we call on Him He will help. He is a very present help in time of trouble. Stay in His Word and pray always.

I can tell you by experiences that having faith in God is the best life you will ever have. Everything won't be perfect but God will be with you and lead you in the path of righteousness. When you are in trouble or have problems come your way He will be there to help you through them. He has been with me all of my life. I can't remember a time in my life that I wasn't aware that He was God. When I accepted Him in my life at the age of 9 and was baptized He was there. Because of my faith in Him and His love for me He has kept me all of these years. He has met me all of my needs and have even given me more than I have needed. He has fed me both spiritually and physically. Without Him keeping me I often wonder where I would be today. I have had some terrible times in my life and most of it was my choices and wrong choosing. But even in that God has kept His hands on me and have forgiven me of all of my wrongs and sins. That's what my Lord will do for you, as long as you have faith in Him for He has no respect of persons. God will give you the desires of your heart if you continue to follow Him and be obedient to Him. The greatest desire of my heart was to have a Christian husband, one who loved God and put

Him first place in his heart and life. God has fulfilled that desire of my heart. He fulfilled that over 25 years ago. I was the one that hindered it so long. Sometimes we are our greatest enemy. We can tie God's hands and hinder his plans for us. As I waited I prayed and continued to work in the ministry that He had called me in. It's not what I done but what He done for me. I give Him all the glory and praise for what He's done for me. He will do what He says. His Word is true and it will never fail and it will never change. God has a plan for each and everyone but sometimes we mess it up but He doesn't give up on us. He knows our heart and our motives. He knows our real desires. I encourage you to try Him, have faith in Him for faith never fails.

Ps.37:3-5, Trust in the Lord and do good and you shall live in the land and be fed. Delight yourself in the Lord and He will give you the desires of your heart. Commit your ways unto the Lord and trust Him and He will bring it to pass. Verse 7, rest in the Lord and wait patiently for Him. God will give us rest and peace if we will have faith in Him. We need to trust Him in everything. Don't try to lean on your own understanding but just trust Him with all of your heart, mind, soul and strength. Verses 23-24, The steps of a good man are ordered by the Lord and they delight in Him and in His ways. If you should fall He will pick you up and hold you in His hand. We all make mistakes because we are still living in this human body. God is there to pick you up and forgive you and help you not to make the same mistake again. Verse 40, God will save you because you trust Him and because of your faith in Him. I John 8-10, John said, if anyone says that he has no sin then you deceive yourselves and the truth is not in you. If we confess our sins then He is faithful and just to forgive us of our sins and cleanse us from all un righteousness. If we confess that we have not sinned then we make Him out to be a liar and His Word has no place in our lives. For all have sinned and fallen short of the glory of God.

We can trust His Word in all things. If we don't doubt He will do all that He said He would do. Thank God for His love, mercy and forgiveness. I thank Him for His patience and steadfastness for me. Please don't let doubt destroy you. Ask God to remove any signs of doubt in your life. David prayed, search me O God and see if there be any evil way in me. We need to pray and ask Him to search our hearts and lives to make sure we have everything in order with Him. Believe on the Lord Jesus Christ and you shall be saved now and forever. Doubt and faith does not mix, you will either have one or the other. That's like having Christ and the devil both living in your heart and life. It can't be, for you have to have one or the other. They both won't live in the same temple. Whom do you serve? Which one is living within you? The devil will never do anything for you except bring you down and carry you with him to hell. Follow Jesus Christ and He will save you and keep you in His care forever as long as you abide in Him. Don't let go of Him for He said, He would never let go of you.

Why not give up and let Jesus take a hold of your life. You can live a victorious life here and now and then eternal life with Him and all of the saints. It's a beautiful life serving Jesus Christ. It's a life that you will never regret. Just think about this, you will never be alone again for He will be with you now and always. Trust and obey Him and do not doubt. Have faith in God for faith is the victory.

Invitation to come to Jesus Christ.

If you do not know Jesus as your Savior and Lord, you can accept Him right now. Call on Him and repent of your sins and ask Him to come into your heart and life and He will save you and forgive you of all your sin. Then you need to get baptized in water with immersing. Let God wash away all of your sins and make you all new in Him. Then get into the Word of God, the Bible, read and study and pray to Him always. Find you a church that teaches the whole truth, the full gospel of Jesus Christ and go every time the doors are opened. You grow and learn by reading and hearing the Word of God. Keep the commandments of God and follow Jesus. Now you have to add works with your faith for faith without works is dead so put your faith to action. You will never regret taking this step of faith. May God bless you and keep you in His will and care always. Amen

Conclusion

Therefore, since we have been made right in God's sight by faith,

we have peace with God because of what Jesus Christ our Lord has

done for us.

Rom. 5: 1 (NLT)

Thou will keep him in perfect peace, whose mind is stayed on

Thee, because he trust in Thee.

Isaiah 26: 3 (KJV)

For the eyes of the Lord are over the righteous and His ears are

Open unto their prayers.

I Pet. 3:12   (KJV)

God is our refuge and strength a very present help in trouble.

Psalms 46:1   (KJV)

About the Author

$\mathcal{I}$ was born in a little place in Virginia called Alton. I was raised in a Christian home and have 5 sisters and I brother. Both of my parents have gone on to be with the Lord. They both were blessed to live long lives together. My mother died at the age of 94 and my dad was 96. I was saved and baptized at the age of 9 in a Baptist church. I was called of God at the age of 11 to do a work for Him but didn't heed the call, to my deepest sorrow and regrets. I was married at an early age, and have 5 wonderful girls. Four of them and I started singing Gospel music when the youngest was only 5. We were able to minister at many churches, nursing homes and other events and places. Anywhere that God opened the door for us we would go. I was always in church, singing in the choir, teaching and directing the youth choir. All of my life I have been singing gospel music with different groups. I always wanted to be in the work of the Lord. I could never be satisfied with doing nothing. My youngest daughter and I had a prison ministry called, Mother and Daughter team. She was only 8 when we started that ministry.

I missed my calling then and I can't turn back the years but I can go forward now in what God has called me to do. God said that He never repents of His calling. I am an ordained minister along with my husband Leon. We are at this time, doing the music ministry at the church that we attend and are a member of in Richmond, Va. We do evangelistic ministry, we preach and sing Southern Gospel music. We go wherever God opens the doors. We have written many songs that we sing. We have been in this ministry for about 26 years. Our names aren't in the bright lights, nor are we famous, but God knows who we are and where our hearts are. He's done so many miracles in our lives. He's kept me from death several times that I know of and I'm sure there were more times. We will never know just what He's kept us from until we see Him face to face and sit down and talk to Him in Glory.

I don't have a PHD, B.A. or a Master's degree in anything but I do have a B.A.H.G,E., Born Again Holy Ghost Experience with God. I like John, received all of my education and teaching from teachers and preachers over the years. The best teacher still, is the Holy Spirit. He will lead and guide you into all truth. I have studied the Word of God for many years and God is still teaching me. I love the Word of God. I believe that God has called me into this writing ministry. He laid a scripture in my heart many years ago and I though it was to write songs for I have written many songs. Psalm 45:1, "My tongue is the pen of a ready writer " I kind of brushed it aside but He would never let me let go of that scripture. I know that the books I have written are ordained and anointed of Him. I will continue to write as long as he gives me the words and the anointing to write for Him. My prayer is that they will bless everyone that reads them as much as they blessed me as I was writing them. They are not about me but about Him, Jesus Christ and what He has done for me and wants to do for you.

I want to thank God for my wonderful Christian husband, Leon, truly a man of God. He puts God above all others and everything, and me second place. That's the way God designs a marriage. God said, If you will delight yourself in Him then He would give you the desires of your heart. God gave me the desire of my heart when He gave me Leon.

You can contact me at, clhmb7@yahoo.com or write, Hilda Marie Barton at 1766 Cook Rd. Powhatan, Va. 23139

Personal notes

Personal notes

Personal notes

Personal notes